"In this engaging and readable book, Derek Tovey uses a narrative-critical approach to Mark's story of Jesus. He shows that, while the story ends abruptly at 16:8, the real ending is in Mark 13. Here the author encourages the rehabilitated disciples, and indeed Mark's readers of every generation, to 'keep awake' until the kingdom of God is established. This is an insightful treatment of Mark's story. It deserves to be widely read."

—PHILIP CHURCH, Senior Lecturer in Biblical Studies, School of Theology Mission and Ministry, Laidlaw College, New Zealand

"Beginning with the troubling original ending of Mark's Gospel, Derek Tovey takes the reader on a journey to discover the identity of Jesus. En route he finds an account of Jesus that gently but firmly leads readers of the Gospel . . . to begin to write their own lives into the story. Backed by non-intrusive scholarship, this highly accessible investigation is filled with insight both on the Gospel of Mark and on the figure of Jesus."

—TIM MEADOWCROFT, Head of School of Theology, Mission and Ministry, Laidlaw College, New Zealand

Read Mark and Learn

Read
MARK
and Learn

Following Mark's Jesus

Derek Tovey

WIPF & STOCK · Eugene, Oregon

READ MARK AND LEARN
Following Mark's Jesus

Copyright © 2014 Derek Tovey. All rights reserved. Except for brief quotations in critical publications or reviews, no part of this book may be reproduced in any manner without prior written permission from the publisher. Write: Permissions. Wipf and Stock Publishers, 199 W. 8th Ave., Suite 3, Eugene, OR 97401.

Wipf & Stock
An Imprint of Wipf and Stock Publishers
199 W. 8th Ave., Suite 3
Eugene, OR 97401

www.wipfandstock.com

ISBN 13: 978-1-62564-138-0

Manufactured in the U.S.A.

New Revised Standard Version Bible: Anglicized Edition, copyright 1989, 1995, Division of Christian Education of the National Council of the Churches of Christ in the United States of America. Used by permission. All rights reserved.

Acknowledgments and thanks to the following for use of quoted material:
To Hymns Ancient & Modern Ltd. for permission to use the Collect for Advent 2, pp. 426–27 of *The Alternative Service Book 1980* (© The Central Board of Finance of the Church of England, 1980).

Extract from "The Hollow Men" taken from *Collected Poems 1909–1962* © Estate of T. S. Eliot and reprinted by permission of Faber & Faber Ltd.

Extract from "The Hollow Men" from *Collected Poems 1909–1962*, by T. S. Eliot. Copyright 1936 by Houghton Mifflin Harcourt Publishing Company. Copyright © renewed by Thomas Stearns Eliot. Reprinted by permission of Houghton Mifflin Harcourt Publishing Company. All rights reserved.

For my mother, Marjorie, and my daughter, Anna,
two who have followed and served Jesus.

Contents

Preface | ix
Acknowledgments | xi

1 Making Sense of Mark's Ending | 1
2 Who Is Jesus? | 22
3 Following Jesus on the Way | 59
4 Mark 13: An "Embedded" End to the Gospel? | 93
Epilogue: Reading Mark's Gospel | 113

Some Suggested Reading on Mark's Gospel | 127
Bibliography | 131

Preface

THE TITLE OF THIS book, *Read Mark and Learn*, is, first of all, an invitation to do just that: to read the Gospel of Mark. My hope in what follows is to show that the Gospel is a connected story. So, even before you read this book, you may wish to read the whole of the Gospel at one sitting. It is about the length of a short novel or a longish short story. In an epilogue, I supply five studies which look at the Gospel under a series of thematic headings. There I provide readings from the Gospel along with questions. You might like to work through these studies first (after you have read the Gospel through!) before you read the book's four chapters.

This book comes out of some previous study done years ago, and also after teaching the Gospel in formal academic settings, and to groups of people in church-related study days, workshops and, in one case, a series of Holy Week talks. I am grateful to students and participants in these classes and study days for the stimulation and insights they provided: and for the opportunity to try some of this material out on them first.

The title of this book was inspired by a prayer in *The Alternative Service Book 1980* of the Church of England. The prayer reads thus:

Preface

> Blessed Lord,
> who caused all holy Scriptures
> to be written for our learning:
> help us so to hear them,
> *to read, mark, learn,* and inwardly digest them
> that, through patience, and the comfort
> of your holy word,
> we may embrace and for ever hold fast
> the hope of everlasting life,
> which you have given us in our Saviour Jesus Christ.[1]

I hope that my book may stimulate and enliven your reading of Mark's Gospel, so that you may learn from it.

---

1. The collect for Advent 2, in the Church of England, *Alternative Service Book 1980*, 426–27, emphasis mine. Some Anglicans and Episcopalians may be familiar with this prayer in its original form in the 1662 *Book of Common Prayer*.

Acknowledgments

THIS BOOK WAS BEGUN while on sabbatical leave in 2010. I want to acknowledge here the support and help given by the St. John's College leadership and the Trust Board in enabling this writing project. Thanks are also due to Professor Elaine Wainwright, the Head of the School of Theology in the University of Auckland. I wish also to acknowledge and thank the School of Theology, University of Auckland and the College of St. John the Evangelist for the financial assistance provided in bringing this book to publication. My daughter, Anna, did some work on the manuscript in preparing it for publication. She also made some suggestions for its improvement. For her help and her advice, I thank her.

1

Making Sense of Mark's Ending

"THIS IS THE WAY the world ends / Not with a bang but a whimper."[1] So wrote T. S. Eliot, concluding his poem, "The Hollow Men." Mark's Gospel begins with a "bang," and ends, not with a whimper, but with silence. The first verse of the Gospel reads: "The beginning of the good news of Jesus Christ, the Son of God."[2] At the conclusion of the Gospel, the reader learns how three women go to the tomb where Jesus is buried early on the first day of the week. When they get there, they find the stone rolled away from the tomb and inside the tomb a young man who tells them that Jesus' body is not there because he has been raised. The women are to go to the disciples and tell them that Jesus has gone ahead of them to Galilee; they will see the

---

1. In *Complete Poems*, 86.

2. All references are quoted from the New Revised Standard Version (NRSV), unless otherwise indicated.

risen Jesus there. Then comes this statement (Mark 16:8): "So they [the women] fled from the tomb, for terror and amazement had seized them; and they said nothing to anyone, for they were afraid."

There is good reason to think that this was the original ending of the Gospel. But, if so, it has left generations of readers feeling puzzled or dissatisfied. Why should the Gospel have concluded on this note of silence and fear? Should it end here? Can it really have ended here? These last two questions will be addressed first, as it will be seen that many readers and scholars of the Gospel have concluded that it did not end at 16:8, and certainly should not. If you look at your Bible, you will see that, in fact, the Gospel does not end at verse 8. There are a further twelve verses, in which Jesus appears to Mary Magdalene, and two other disciples, and finally the eleven, whom he upbraids for not believing the reports of his resurrection. Then Jesus ascends to heaven, while the disciples go out and proclaim "the good news everywhere, while the Lord worked with them and confirmed the message by the signs that accompanied it" (16:20).

The problem is that it would seem that these verses were added to the Gospel later. They are not part of the Gospel as originally written. You may find that your Bible has a heading such as "The Longer Ending of Mark" above verses 9 to 20. You will probably find another heading reading, "The Shorter Ending of Mark," with some such text as: "And all that had been commanded them they told briefly to those around Peter. And afterward Jesus himself sent out through them, from east to west, the sacred and imperishable proclamation of eternal salvation."

The evidence of the ancient manuscripts of Mark's Gospel is that Mark 16:9–20 are missing from two of the oldest Greek manuscripts (called Codex Sinaiticus and

Making Sense of Mark's Ending

Codex Vaticanus), and from numerous other manuscripts. Moreover a number of early church fathers (such as Clement of Alexandria and Origen) do not appear to be aware of the existence of these verses, and others such as Eusebius and Jerome indicate that the verses are not in copies of Mark known to them.[3] Other manuscripts that include them also include the shorter ending; and yet others include the verses with notes and marks in the margins of the manuscripts which indicate that the copyist is aware that these verses are not original to the Gospel. One old manuscript has only the shorter ending of the Gospel.

Hence, the manuscript evidence is mixed but suggests to scholars that the "Longer Ending" and the "Shorter Ending" have been added to the Gospel later. They stand as testimony to the fact that early readers also found that the conclusion of the Gospel at 16:8 was unsatisfactory. There is also a grammatical reason for considering that 16:8 should not be the conclusion of the Gospel. In the Greek the verse concludes with the conjunction, *gar*, translated into English as "for." While it is possible to conclude a sentence or a paragraph with the word *gar*, for a long time the argument went that a whole book could not end in this manner. This presupposes that there must have been something to follow the *gar*. We may get a sense of this expectation if we translate the last clause not as "for they were afraid," but "they were afraid for . . ."

A number of scholars have brought forward evidence and arguments to show that it was indeed possible to end a lengthy piece of writing, or a book, with a final *gar*. The objections of an earlier generation of scholars to such an ending have, therefore, been somewhat set aside, though the issue has not been finally settled. Nevertheless, this grammatical issue, together with the strange, open-ended

3. Metzger, *Textual Commentary*, 102–3.

conclusion that 16:8 brings to the Gospel, has led many scholars to believe that the ending is unfinished, or perhaps lost.

How can this have happened? It has been suggested that the author of the Gospel was unable to finish because he fell ill, or died, or was arrested. Alternatively, some have suggested that the end was deliberately cut or torn away. A more plausible suggestion is that the ending of the Gospel has been accidentally lost. This is especially possible if the Gospel first appeared in codex form as this is more like our modern book than the papyrus scroll: in this case, it is conceivable that the final page (or pages) became detached and lost.[4]

The difficulty with accepting that the ending was lost is that the loss must have happened early, that is, before

---

4. A codex was made by taking sheets of papyrus, and folding them in half: several such sheets were generally bound together. Parchment was also used, but it seems that papyrus codices were more likely to have been used in the first and second centuries. While there is some question as to when codices replaced papyrus scrolls as the preferred medium for producing books, a reasonably strong case can be made for accepting that this occurred sometime in the first century, particularly as far as Christian writings are concerned. In fact, it might be a moot point whether it would be more likely for the final page of a codex to be lost than for the end of a scroll to be lost through degeneration. It seems likely that early Christian works would have been written on "single-quire" codices, that is, a single collection of papyrus sheets, gathered together by inserting one sheet inside another, and stitching the whole lot together along the folded edge (and the earliest Christian codices would have been more like a pamphlet than a book). A single-quire codex would be reasonably robust, and if the stitching came apart, one would expect the outer papyrus sheet to fall away, which would result in loss as much in the front of the codex as at the end. When all is said and done, postulating the loss of the final page(s) of Mark's Gospel is as speculative as other theories. On the making and development of the use of codices in early Christianity, see Gamble, *Books and Readers*. A briefer account may be found in his article, "Codex," 1067–69.

Making Sense of Mark's Ending

other copies that retained the ending as it had been, were made. No manuscripts containing the supposed lost ending have ever been found. Both the "Longer" and the "Shorter" endings found in the manuscripts, or versions of the Bible, strike readers and scholars as attempts to patch up the ending that has supposedly been lost; or, of course, simply to supply another ending.

There is a further consideration. It is difficult to continue smoothly beyond the end of 16:8. The little phrase "they said nothing to anyone" provides a "road block" that is difficult to get around. One either has to ignore it, or alter it in some way, in order to proceed. Scholars generally accept that both the Gospels of Matthew and Luke depend upon Mark as one of their sources. It is interesting to see how they each deal with the problem. Both ignore the statement "they said nothing to anyone," but Matthew retains the idea of fear: "So they left the tomb quickly with fear and great joy, and ran to tell his disciples" (Matt 28:8). Luke, changing the messenger who delivers the news of the resurrection to "two men in dazzling clothes," moves directly from their words (also changed from Mark's version) to the response of the women, which is to remember Jesus' prophecy of his resurrection (see, e.g., Luke 9:22), and go from the tomb to tell "all this to the eleven and all the rest" (Luke 24:8–9).

These, and other, considerations have caused many readers, certainly an increasing number of scholars in recent years, to conclude that the writer of Mark's Gospel intended to end his account of "the good news" at chapter 16, verse 8. This is the position I adopt in this book. I invite you to read this book, and the Gospel with that assumption in mind. The writer deliberately and intentionally ended this Gospel with an emphasis on the fear and the silence of the women. Now, in the end, you may make up your own mind about whether or not the Gospel was originally intended to end in this fashion. I cannot entirely rule out the possibility that something has happened to leave the Gospel in this state. But, as I hope to show, I think that fruitful readings of the Gospel may result when one accepts that the writer ended the story at Mark 16:8.

REASONS FOR ENDING THE GOSPEL AT 16:8

Once one accepts that the most likely original ending of Mark's Gospel is the statement that the women run from the tomb, in fear and amazement, and say nothing to anyone because they are afraid, one is faced with an interesting and complex question: "Why did the writer choose to end the story like this?" The answers to this have been many and various. I am going to outline a number of possible answers here. Some may be mutually exclusive; but in other cases, it may be possible to hold together a number of answers, or better, reasons for the ending. Many contemporary readers of the Gospel are finding that it is possible to have multiple readings of the story. It is not necessarily a matter of settling upon one "right" reading, but of asking how does this reading help make sense of this story? Perhaps just as important are the questions: how does this reading help me make sense of this story and what impact might this reading have upon the way in which I respond to the story?

At the outset, it is worth being clear about what is and what is not missing from Mark's ending. The news of Jesus' resurrection is most definitely present in the words of the young man in the tomb: "Do not be alarmed: you are looking for Jesus of Nazareth, who was crucified. He has been raised; he is not here" (16:6). What is not recounted is an account of an appearance by Jesus to anyone: either to the women or to anyone else. But an appearance is promised: "But go, tell his disciples and Peter that he is going ahead of

Making Sense of Mark's Ending

you to Galilee: there you will see him just as he told you" (16:7). Mark 16:8 leaves the reader with the impression that the message did not get to the disciples. Thus the reader is left with the question: "If the women did not tell the disciples of Jesus' resurrection, who did?"

Also, it is as well to recall that by the time Mark's Gospel was read, or heard (and we must return to this thought later), the news of Jesus' resurrection, including stories of the appearance of the risen Jesus, had been preached and taught around the Mediterranean world for thirty to forty years. Assuming, as is most likely, that the original audience for Mark's Gospel would have been Christians, we may take it that they would have heard this story secure in the knowledge both that Jesus had been raised from the dead, and that he had appeared to a number of people. So, their reaction to the news of the women's failure to pass on the message would have been to understand that if the women did not deliver the message, others must have.

Perhaps the ending of Mark's Gospel was a way of undermining the witness of the women to the resurrection. The implication is that the news of the resurrection was first published not by women but by others, most likely the male disciples of Jesus. In a society that did not place much value on the word of a woman, this may have been reassuring. Indeed, in Jewish society, the witness of women was discounted, and disallowed in a court of law. Hence, Mark's Gospel suggests, not women but men were really responsible for the message of the resurrection being spread abroad.

The trouble with this hypothesis is that, if this was the writer's intention, it did not really work. Or, it was only persuasive for a while, and then only locally. I say this because both Matthew and Luke, whom you recall used Mark as a source, had no compunction in attributing the bearing of the initial message of Jesus' resurrection to women. Nor, of course did the writer of John's Gospel. This suggests that the tradition of women bearing news of Jesus' resurrection to the disciples was deeply rooted and too strong to be effectively countered. It is true that our earliest record of the resurrection appearances in the New Testament, that of Paul in 1 Corinthians 15:3–8, makes no mention of appearances to women, nor of angelic messages to women at the tomb. But Paul's purposes here are different from the Gospel writers'; and he may well be drawing on what had become something of a creedal statement among early Christians. The evidence of all the Gospels is that women played an important part in receiving (and as far as the other Gospels are concerned, in passing on) the message of the resurrection. Certainly, they were central to the events of that first Easter day. It might possibly be part of the strategy of Mark's ending to discredit the women's testimony, or even, in some subtle way, to devalue their role. But it does not seem likely.

Another way of understanding Mark's ending is to focus on the women's reaction to the young man's words. The text says that "they went out and fled from the tomb, for terror and amazement had seized them." The terror and amazement here arises from the women's experience of the numinous. Here they are faced with an event that is frightening and confusing: an empty tomb, a missing body, and a strange young man with an even stranger message. But more than that: they are faced with a situation that is as mysterious as it is puzzling. Indeed, if they understand the young man to be a messenger from God (and many scholars believe that the description of the young man is intended to evoke the understanding that he is an angel), then they are also experiencing an event brought about by God. They are fleeing, if you will, "holy ground."

Making Sense of Mark's Ending

Some years ago, I read a book by Barbara Smith called *Poetic Closure*. In it she writes about a "kinesthetic image" which is "not a picture of the event from the outside, but a sense of what it feels like to be engaged in it."[5] What the writer of Mark's Gospel gives the reader in the ending of his Gospel, then, is a kinesthetic image. The reader is not only told of the women's visit to the tomb, but is also given a sense of what it must have been like to have been there on that momentous yet confusing morning. In the abrupt and shocking ending, the reader enters into the same sense of confusion and wonder that the women must have felt on that day.

Throughout the Gospel, the author has provided instances of fear, of wonder, and of amazement in the face of Jesus' actions and his teaching (see, e.g., 1:27; 2:12; 5:42b). A particularly striking example is found at the conclusion of Mark 4, when panicked disciples in the midst of a storm are "filled with great awe" when Jesus stills the storm, and brings calm. Here, at the conclusion of the Gospel, is another instance: in the face of news of the resurrection, the women are overcome with holy terror and amazement: they are struck dumb and can only flee from the tomb overcome. But do they never recover? And given that they say nothing to anyone, can their fear really be a fear of the numinous? Are they to remain in a catatonic state forever? In terms of the writer's strategy, the answer seems to be "Yes." But it does not seem possible that they should remain so, nor does it seem satisfactory. There must be some other purpose.

---

5. Smith, *Poetic Closure*, 178.

DISCREDITED DISCIPLES?

The ending of Mark's Gospel is intended to discredit, not the women, but Jesus' male disciples. Mark's Gospel presents a negative picture of the disciples, and, as the Gospel story proceeds, they fail ever more disastrously to be faithful followers of Jesus. Often they are portrayed as misunderstanding Jesus, and as Jesus moves toward his death, they progress toward complete failure: Judas betrays Jesus, Peter denies him, all the disciples flee from the Garden of Gethsemane leaving Jesus to face crucifixion alone. No male disciples are said to witness Jesus' death, not even from a distance as do some of Jesus' female followers (see 14:40–41). No male disciple sees where Jesus is buried. In the end, even the women fail, so that the disciples never get the message about meeting Jesus in Galilee. They are not reunited with Jesus, they are not rehabilitated as disciples, and so they remain discredited.

This is the view of Theodore Weeden in his 1971 book, *Mark—Traditions in Conflict*. Weeden traces the way in which the Gospel presents the disciples in an increasingly negative light. In the early chapters they come across as imperceptive, not really understanding much of Jesus' teaching, and struggling to grasp who he is. Then, about the middle of the Gospel, near Caesarea Philippi, Jesus asks the disciples who they think he is, and receives this reply from Peter: "You are the Messiah" (in the Greek, *Christos*, Christ; see 8:29).

But it transpires that Peter and the other disciples do not really understand what it means for Jesus to be the Messiah. When Jesus tries to teach them that messiahship means that he must go the way of suffering and the cross (in three "passion predictions"; see 8:31; 9:31; 10:33–34), they misunderstand him. Thus they move from imperception to

Making Sense of Mark's Ending

misconception: and no matter how hard Jesus tries, they continue in their misunderstanding. Finally, they reject Jesus: they all abandon him and flee (14:50). And that is where the story leaves them. They are never reconciled and reunited with Jesus. The promise made in 14:28 that, after Jesus has been raised from death, he will go before them into Galilee where they will be reunited with him, is never fulfilled. The disciples never receive the message. The fact that the young man gives the women a message which is never delivered, according to the Gospel's ending, is the author's way of finally and fully pulling the rug out from under the disciples' feet. Weeden shows how the author does this by taking an "empty tomb story" traditionally comprised of 16:2, 5, 6, 8a and adding verses 1 and 7 (where the promise of a meeting is reiterated) and verse 8b ("and they said nothing to anyone, for they were afraid"), which undercuts the expected "happy ending."

Why should the author wish to portray the disciples in this way, to leave them utterly discredited at the conclusion of the Gospel? The reason lies in what Weeden perceives to be the background situation that the Gospel is addressing. In the Christian community of which the writer is a part there is a christological dispute raging over the nature of Jesus and the character of his messiahship. The disciples are made to represent those whom the writer is opposing, while Jesus and the narrator (who is, of course, the mouthpiece of the writer) represent the correct Christology that Mark wants to put forward.

The position which the opponents hold, and which is illustrated in the portrayal of the disciples, is that Jesus is a kind of wonder-working divine man. The first part of the Gospel sets out this kind of understanding, which is why Jesus is portrayed as doing lots of miracles which arouse much wonder and admiration. When Peter proclaims that Jesus is the Messiah, his statement is based on the understanding gained to that point, namely, that Jesus is a wonder-worker, and a kind of "divine-man." Jesus then puts forward the correct understanding that he is to be a suffering Messiah.

Not only do the opponents, represented by the disciples, have a wrong conception of the Christ, and messiahship, but they also do not understand the true nature of discipleship. They have an enthusiastic, charismatic type of understanding that puts emphasis on the fact that they, too, can work wonders, and that they can have an immediate relationship with the risen Jesus. But they do not have time for the suffering, and servant-like discipleship, such as Jesus emulated and taught. Weeden writes:

> Like Paul's . . . opponents [in 2 Corinthians], they have become enamored of what attracts man: the miracle-working capacity of Jesus. They have ignored the most important aspect of Jesus, that which God ordains: his suffering servanthood. The same results obtain when Jesus tries to persuade them to suffering discipleship. Again thinking like man, they want the glory, honor, the sense of self-exaltation, authority, superiority, and veneration from peers that the ["divine-man"] wants (9:33–41; 10:13–16, 35–45). Sacrificial discipleship (10:17–27) or discipleship without its tangible rewards (10:28–29, 35–40) is incomprehensible to the disciples.[6]

---

6. Weeden, *Traditions*, 68. Weeden relates the disciples' position to what he calls a *theios anēr* (which may be translated "divine man") Christology. He maintains that belief in "divine men" was current in the wider society in which the early church took root, and influenced the view of Christ among certain elements within early Christianity. My summary here is a rather bald way of putting what is a complex and much-debated argument.

Making Sense of Mark's Ending

The clue that this position represents that of people within the Markan community (or the life of the church with which the author is involved) is found in Mark 13:6, 22 where it says that people will come in Jesus' name saying "I am he," and that false messiahs and false prophets (for which read "the opponents") will appear doing signs and wonders "to lead astray, if possible, the elect." The writer tells his story to undercut the position of these "false prophets" by discrediting the disciples in the eyes of the reader, and by presenting the correct christological view in the teaching of Jesus.

Two other scholarly readers of Mark's Gospel who see a clue to the purpose of the writer in the negative portrayal of disciples are John Dominic Crossan and Werner H. Kelber. Crossan adopts a redactional-critical approach to the Gospel, as does Weeden.[7] But Crossan focuses on the women disciples in the crucifixion-resurrection story, whom he links with the portrayal of Jesus' family ("mother, brothers and sisters") in Mark 3:20–35 and 6:1–6, who in turn become linked with those who oppose Jesus.[8] He notes that one of the women mentioned among the women disciples is named as being Mary, the mother of Joses, as well as James (see Mark 15:40, 47; 16:1), and Crossan argues that this is an addition to underline the fact that this Mary is the Mary referred to in 6:3, and, therefore, the mother of Jesus. These women disciples, then, represent the church in Jerusalem (James, Mary's son and Jesus' brother, was an important leader of this church), which is also associated

---

7. Redaction criticism is a method that examines the "editorial" activity of a gospel writer. It attends to the way in which an evangelist has used sources and traditions, and how these have been ordered and arranged to shape the particular theological themes and ideas that the evangelist wishes to convey to the reader.

8. Crossan, "Mark and the Relatives of Jesus," 81–113.

with Peter, James and John. This church has a mistaken understanding of Jesus and it is also in a jurisdictional debate with the Markan church. Thus, the Gospel of Mark discredits both the doctrinal position and the authority of the Jerusalem church.

Werner H. Kelber, who reads the Gospel as the "single coherent story" of a "dramatically plotted journey,"[9] makes the point that "each evangelist reinterprets the life of Jesus for his own time and people."[10] The time this Gospel relates to is post-70 CE, after the Roman-Jewish war when the temple in Jerusalem was destroyed. The evangelist writes a story that seems to criticize and attack the Jerusalem church and community, represented in the Gospel by the Twelve, especially the "Three" (Peter, James, and John), Jesus' family, and the Galilean women (Mark 15:40, 41). The Twelve and the Galilean women have failed in their discipleship and Jesus rejects his family. "Jesus' closest followers failed to understand the nature of the Galilean community, abandoned Jesus, missed his coronation on the cross [having run away], and were thus stalled in Jerusalem, never reaching the goal of Galilee."[11] The evangelist's disagreement with the Jerusalem church is seen in his attitude toward mission to the Gentiles, which he promotes; his insistence on the abolition of ritual taboos (see, e.g., Mark 7:14–23); and a focus on the death of Jesus in weakness and abandonment on the cross.

In the latter part of the Gospel, the narrator recounts the desertion of all the disciples: and the ending of the Gospel suggests the downfall of the disciples and not their rehabilitation. In Jerusalem, Jesus makes it clear that Jerusalem and the temple are not the place of the kingdom,

9. See Kelber, *Mark's Story*, 11, 9.
10. Ibid., 88.
11. Ibid., 90.

Making Sense of Mark's Ending

rather Galilee is the final destination. Kelber argues that, after the disappearance of the male disciples, the women who come to the tomb "acting in the place of the disciples, bring the disciples' tragedy to its logical conclusion."[12] As the women never deliver the message to the disciples, these latter remain in Jerusalem where they wait for the kingdom to come in power. "The Kingdom community in Galilee will not be represented by the disciples."[13]

The fact that Mark's Gospel is written post-70 CE means not that he is seeking to "pronounce judgment on the mother church as much as [to provide] an explanation for its extinction."[14] The evangelist has his readers relive the story of Jesus so that they may understand that Jesus announced the arrival of the kingdom away from Jerusalem in Galilee. The disciples are portrayed as failing to understand Jesus' mission and purpose. This is the cause of the crisis in Jerusalem, but the readers are challenged to understand that it is they who must carry on the imperatives of the gospel. They must fulfill the commission to take the gospel to all nations, to establish a kingdom in which the values of love for God and neighbor override all rules and regulations, and a kingdom that promotes not hierarchical but egalitarian structures. They are to follow the way of Jesus in "service and suffering on behalf of others, not the art of self-aggrandizement."[15]

---

12. Ibid., 87.
13. Ibid.
14. Ibid., 91.
15. Ibid., 94.

FAILED DISCIPLES NOT DISCREDITED BUT REHABILITATED

Another scholarly reader of Mark's Gospel, Norman Petersen, draws a distinction between the Gospel's story time and its plotted time.[16] Story time is time as conceived by the story as a whole, the ordering of the total world of the story and the chronological ordering of the events within that world. The reader obtains story time from the information given in the story. In Mark's Gospel story time, by and large, runs from the beginning of Jesus' ministry which is signaled in Mark by the appearance of John the Baptist in the wilderness and the baptism of Jesus through to the death and resurrection of Jesus (or to the discovery of the empty tomb). But the reader learns that there are also other events that happen outside of that time frame (though, in a sense, they are still part of the overall story time). For example, the first verses refer to a prophecy that was made some time before the appearance of John the Baptist and is now being fulfilled. In Mark 13, Jesus tells four disciples of some events that are going to happen in the future (beyond the end of the Gospel's story time).

Plotted time, on the other hand, refers to the order of the events as they are actually arranged and told by the narrator. This order may not exactly be the same as the order the reader imagines things to have happened in terms of the world of the story. So, for example, the reader is told that Jesus begins his ministry after John has been arrested (1:14), so the reader assumes this must have taken place at some time between the time that Jesus is baptized by John and the time Jesus begins his preaching in Galilee. But it is not until Mark 6:17–29, that the reader is told the story of that arrest

---

16. For what follows, I am drawing on Petersen, *Literary Criticism*, ch. 3. See also his, "When Is the End," 151–66.

Making Sense of Mark's Ending

and, in fact, discovers that John has also been beheaded (6:16) and how this came about. That is, the death of John is plotted out of sequence, as it were, and the reader learns about it through a kind of flashback. The reason that the reader is told of the "out-of-sequence" event at this point in the story, is because news of Jesus' activities is spreading, so that King Herod has heard about him and thinks that he must be John the Baptist raised from the dead.

Even more important, for the reader's understanding of the story, is the fact that intimations are given of events that will happen in the future. Some of these are fulfilled in the plotting of the story, and others are not. So, for instance, Jesus predicts his betrayal and death at the hands of the authorities, and this prediction is, of course, fulfilled in the final chapters of the Gospel. Jesus also predicts that Peter will deny him, and this is also fulfilled. He further predicts that all the disciples will abandon him and flee: Mark 14:50–52 starkly reports this, and imaginatively symbolizes it.

The fulfillment of some of Jesus' predictions, Petersen argues, raises the expectation that all of his predictions will be fulfilled. Therefore the reader assumes that those which are not fulfilled by the time the story ends (at 16:8) will be fulfilled at some future time beyond the end of the plotted story. The effect of this is to suggest to the reader that the prediction Jesus makes in Mark 14:28, that after he is raised from death (on the third day) he will go ahead of the disciples into Galilee, a prediction that is reiterated by the young man in the tomb, will be fulfilled beyond the end of the story. In other words, the reader is invited to imaginatively finish the story by understanding that the predicted meeting does take place in Galilee, but not within plotted time. So the disciples do meet Jesus and are reinstated as faithful disciples. This turns the ending into an ironic and open ending (not a literal ending): it puts a hopeful spin on the fact that, for example, Peter is singled out for special mention and suggests that his denial of Jesus is not going to result in a permanent rift (Peter's tears, 14:72, have already served to maintain the reader's sympathy with Peter).

There is another feature of the plotted time that serves to underline the fact that the disciples are eventually reinstated as faithful disciples of Jesus. This feature is the presence of chapter 13, where within story time Jesus, before his death, talks about the post-resurrection experience of the disciples, and the persecutions and trials they will face on Jesus' account. Jesus also points forward to his eventual *Parousia*, that is, his appearing again at the end of the age. This means, argues Petersen, that the real end of the story becomes not the resurrection of Jesus but his future *Parousia*. In a sense, chapter 13 is the end of the Gospel, but it has been plotted earlier than the narrative end. So the Gospel of Mark, by its ending, really opens out into the time of the disciples after the resurrection when they are to live and witness faithfully to Jesus, and to wait expectantly for the end. You will find that I pick up Petersen's ideas later in this book as I develop my own reading.

THE END OF THE GOSPEL AS A TURN TO THE READER

Many contemporary readers of Mark's Gospel see the ending as a device on the part of the writer to draw the reader into the story. The open-ended, surprising, seemingly unfinished and unsatisfactory ending prompts the reader to finish the story in some way (we have seen that at least two ancient readers were prompted actually to provide an ending). The ending of the Gospel, then, provides what may be called a turn to the reader and elicits a response from the reader.

Making Sense of Mark's Ending

Here it is important to draw attention to the fact that in the first century, many of those who first encountered Mark's Gospel did not read it for themselves. Rather, they would have heard it read by someone else. In recent years, a number of scholars have stressed the nature of the Gospel as oral and aural. That is, the Gospel would have been presented orally to an audience; indeed, one might even imagine that it was performed. It was heard, rather than read, by the majority of those for whom it was written. It would have continued to have been received aurally as it spread around the ancient Christian world.

One might imagine an early Christian audience (perhaps a congregation in a church) listening intently and expectantly as a reader read the Gospel to them. Expectations would mount as the reader drew toward the end of the story, and embarked on the account of the women's visit to the tomb. The reader would read the words "And they said nothing to anyone, for they were afraid," and stop reading. How would the audience respond? I imagine that there would be a stunned silence for a moment. Someone might then shout out: "Is that it? What happened next?" That would certainly afford an opportunity for the reader, or someone else to explain what happened next. But I like to think that what might have happened was that the audience erupted into a hubbub as members shared with each other the "ending" of the story that they already knew so well.

Be that as it may, a careful reading of the Gospel's story, I suggest, shows that it is structured in such a way to raise questions in the reader's mind. One certainly is, "Why has the writer chosen to end his story in this way?" I have already discussed above a number of ways in which scholars have attempted to answer that question: and there are many more that might have been offered.

There are two questions (which might also be called themes) that the Gospel addresses in the way in which it has been plotted. One is the question about Jesus' identity: who he is. The first part of the Gospel is structured by (among other themes) the question of who Jesus is, and the kinds of reaction and responses evoked by what he does and says. At the halfway point in the story, Jesus himself asks a couple of questions of the disciples: "Who do people say that I am?" and "Who do you say that I am?" (8:27b, 29a). We explore the answer to this latter question in the next chapter. The other is the question about what it means to follow Jesus: how one should be a disciple. In the next two chapters I am going to show how the Gospel develops each of these themes, namely, that of Jesus' identity and of discipleship.

But before I do, I want to suggest to you that the Gospel's ending raises a big question mark—or, perhaps, two question marks—that relate to these themes. As a reader reads Mark's Gospel, he or she will notice that the characters who observe Jesus' actions and hear his teaching are moved to ask questions about him and his teaching. "What is this? A new teaching with authority!" (1:27). "Why does this fellow speak this way? It is blasphemy!" (2:7). A particularly telling question is asked by the disciples at the end of chapter 4: "Who then is this, that even the wind and the sea obey him?" (4:41).

But it might be noted that the question at the end of Mark 4 has no direct answer. Now, I suggest, the ending of the Gospel implicitly raises another question of a similar sort. As the women run from the tomb, dumbstruck and fearful, might not this question be racing through their minds? "If Jesus can be raised from the dead, who can he be?" Whether or not the women might ask that question, I feel sure it is one that the author would have his reader ask: "In the light of the announcement of the resurrection, who can Jesus be?" The author has an answer to hand for this question, and it stands right at the start of his story: "The beginning of the gospel of Jesus Christ, the Son of God."

The other big question mark relates to the theme of discipleship. We have begun to see how this Gospel portrays a history of failure on the part of the disciples in the story. The open-ended conclusion to this story of failing disciples, with its turn to the reader, poses the question: "And what about you? How will you respond to Jesus and the call to proclaim the gospel?"

2

Who Is Jesus?

"THE BEGINNING OF THE good news of Jesus Christ, the Son of God" (Mark 1:1). With these words the narrator begins the story he will tell in this Gospel. I have described the Gospel as beginning with a "bang" because it is forceful and to the point. Yet it also provides readers with something of a puzzle. Should this sentence be understood as functioning as a title for the whole story, or is it simply the start of the story? And if it is the start of the story, to what does "the beginning" refer? Does it simply refer to the preaching of John the Baptist, introduced as it is with a reference to a prophecy in "Isaiah"[1]; or does it refer to the whole of the Gospel; is this entire story in fact the beginning of the good news about Jesus?

While scholars debate the meaning and function of this opening sentence, it, along with the first thirteen verses, which are described as the prologue to the story, provides

---

1. This prophecy is, in fact, a conflation of Old Testament texts; see the discussion below p. 32.

Who Is Jesus?

the reader with a lot of information about Jesus. Thus, the reader embarks upon a reading of the Gospel with much information about the character Jesus, which can guide and direct how the story is received. I shall draw on the information provided in this prologue to describe how the implied author answers the question raised by his Gospel: who is Jesus?[2]

The first thing that the reader learns about the main character in this story is that his name is Jesus. In several places in the Gospel where the narrator or other characters call Jesus by his name, they identify him as "Jesus of [or from] Nazareth" (see 1:24; 10:47; 14:67; 16:6). Thus, in the story Jesus is also identified with reference to his home town: Nazareth. This is where he comes from to be baptized by John (1:9), and it is specifically designated as his "hometown" in Mark 6:1, where his family lives and where, sadly, he finds that he is not held in any high regard. Nazareth is a town in Galilee, and we shall have to return to the significance of Galilee for this story later.

---

2. In the first chapter I referred to the author of the Gospel either as "the author" or "the writer," and occasionally as "the evangelist." In the remainder of this book, I shall refer to "the implied author." This is a term employed by many scholars who read the Gospel using the tools of narrative criticism. The implied author is the image of the author that is embedded in the text, and conceived by the reader in reading the text. In a narrative, there is always a "voice" that tells the story: the "voice" is the narrator. But directing the voice (and responsible for the creation of the narrator), there is a mind (or a "hand") that has determined how the story will be told, and how it will be constructed. The reader senses the presence of this "mind/hand" and conceives a mental image of this organizing presence: the implied author.

JESUS THE CHRIST

In the opening sentence the name Jesus is followed by another name, "Christ." While for many readers today this might appear to be another proper name, indeed it might be taken as a surname, it is really a title, or the description of a role. The word "Christ" is the English form of the Greek, *Christos*, which is itself a translation of a Hebrew word, *Mashiach*, or in English, Messiah. Hence, in this sentence, we might read "the good news about Jesus Messiah" or even "Jesus, the Messiah." Messiah means "anointed" or "anointed one" and refers to the fact that the Messiah would be one anointed by God to fulfill a particular function. In the Old Testament, an adjectival form was used generally of kings, who were anointed as God's vice-regents over Israel, though occasionally priests and prophets were also designated as God's "anointed." In the time of the New Testament, the idea had crystallized, among some Jewish groups and in some writings, into the expectation of a particular figure who was to come as "the Messiah" to establish God's kingdom. What the Gospel's implied author understood in using this term must be determined by reading his story.

In Mark's Gospel many other titles and descriptors are used for Jesus, but that the implied author regards "Christ" as an important designation for Jesus is seen not only in the fact that it appears in this opening sentence, but also by the fact that when it next appears it is used by Peter to answer the question put by Jesus: "Who do you say that I am?" This occurs about halfway through the story, at Mark 8:29[3], and

---

3. A range of ancient manuscripts include the title "Christ" in Mark 1:34, which would have Jesus telling the demons not to say anything because they know he is the Christ (or, Messiah). However, the title occurs in these manuscripts almost certainly because it was added later by a copyist, or copyists; see Metzger, *Textual Commentary*, 64. See also the comments on the eight uses of "Christ" in the

Who Is Jesus?

is seen by many scholars as a major turning point in the narrative. We shall explore the significance of this designation for Jesus shortly, but first we must notice an interesting feature of the way in which the implied author develops his story.

The first sentence conveys information to which the reader is privy, but the characters within the story do not have access to the same understanding of Jesus' identity. Consequently, the story's plot (especially in the first part of the story) hinges around the question of this identity. As Jesus begins his teaching and healing activity his fame spreads. At the same time, questions arise about his identity and the source of his healing power and his authority. For instance, one of the first things Jesus does is to exorcise an evil spirit from a man on a Sabbath day in Capernaum (1:21–28). This amazes the crowd that witness the event and they say to one another: "What is this? A new teaching— with authority! He commands even the unclean spirits and they obey him" (v. 27). When Jesus returns to Capernaum some days later he heals a paralyzed man, but before doing so tells him his sins are forgiven. This prompts some scribes sitting there to ask themselves: "Why does this fellow speak in this way? It is blasphemy! Who can forgive sins but God alone?" (2:7). When, at Jesus' command, the paralyzed man picks up the mat he has been lying on and walks away, the crowd looking on is amazed. They glorify God, saying, "We have never seen anything like this!" (2:12).

Frequently, the narrator informs the reader that Jesus' fame is spreading and that crowds gather around him on many occasions (1:28, 45; 2:2; 3:7–8; 4:1; 5:21; 6:31b, 53–56). Often, the reaction of the crowd, or those witnessing an event, is recorded. Sometimes the assessment of what Jesus says and does is positive (7:37), at other times it is negative

---

Gospel by Broadhead, *Naming Jesus*, 149.

or mixed (3:7, 21, 22, 30; 6:2–3): and the narrator's comment about the reaction of the onlookers to many of Jesus' actions is that they are "amazed" (1:27; 2:12; 5:20, 42b). At the conclusion of Mark 4, after Jesus has calmed a violent windstorm that had sprung up while he and the disciples were in a boat on Lake Galilee, the disciples ask a significant question: "Who then is this, that even the wind and the sea obey him?" (4:41). No answer is given to this question in the narrative: perhaps the reader is invited thereby to ponder his or her own answer. We shall have occasion to return to this episode later.

The upshot of these accounts of the questioning and the reactions of other characters to Jesus' words and actions is to create a theme that focuses on the question of Jesus' identity. So it is that the implied author has Jesus quiz his disciples, at about midpoint in the story, as to people's conclusions about who he is. He asks them: "Who do people say that I am?" (8:27b). There is a range of ideas, apparently, and the disciples rehearse them for Jesus: "John the Baptist; and others, Elijah; and still others, one of the prophets" (8:28; this answer echoes an earlier report on people's opinions by the narrator, see 6:14–16). Jesus then asks the disciples: "But who do you say that I am?" (8:29a). It is at this point that Peter says: "You are the Messiah." (v. 29b).

There is no doubt that Peter's identification of Jesus as the Messiah (or, the Christ) is correct from the implied author's perspective. It echoes the words of the narrator about Jesus in Mark 1:1. Furthermore, Jesus does not gainsay or correct Peter's statement. But what he does do points to a puzzle in this story about how the theme of Jesus' identity is developed: for Jesus sternly orders the disciple not to tell anyone about his identity (8:30). This is not the first time that Jesus has done this. Indeed, while the people at large have a variety of opinions about who Jesus is, there is one

Who Is Jesus?

group that consistently and loudly proclaim his true identity. These are the people who are possessed of evil spirits: in fact, as the narrator points out in 1:34, it is the demons who possess their unfortunate human hosts who are able to identify Jesus. Jesus just as consistently shuts the demons up, curing the possessed person of their demon possession at the same time.

It is the fact that Jesus prevents the demons from identifying him, or shuts them up when they do, as well as the fact that on a number of occasions he tries to prevent people who have been healed from spreading the news about his healing activity (see, e.g., 1:43–44; 5:43; 7:36; and by implication at 8:26), that has led scholars to speak about the "messianic secret." It should be noted in passing that the demons never identify Jesus as "the Christ." It is possible that other reasons might be given why Jesus does not wish healed persons to broadcast the news of their healing. Nonetheless, it is most certainly the case that when Peter identifies Jesus as the Christ, he and all the disciples are sworn to secrecy.

The idea of "the messianic secret" was first proposed by a German scholar William Wrede in a book called *Das Messiasgeheimnis in den Evangelien*, published in 1901.[4] Wrede's view was that the historical Jesus had never proclaimed himself the Messiah during his life. However, after the resurrection, the disciples came to understand that Jesus was indeed the Messiah: though his messiahship was something to be achieved in the future (at the *Parousia*). The evangelist who wrote the Gospel of Mark, perhaps building upon prior traditions, presented the view that Jesus had indeed taught that he was the Messiah, but the reason why this was not widely known was because Jesus

---

4. The English title is *The Messianic Secret* (translated by J. C. G. Grieg).

had instructed the disciples to keep his messiahship secret until after the resurrection.

This theory has been subjected to critique and much modification since it was first proposed by Wrede. For one thing, a reading of the Gospel story suggests that in a number of cases, when he had healed someone, Jesus did not require silence of the fact, nor was he successful in preventing others from spreading the news. Moreover, it is not clear that healing people led inevitably to the conclusion that Jesus was the Messiah. In fact, the story itself indicates that a number of other views on Jesus' identity were held. Some scholars, therefore, conclude that the function of enjoining silence on some of those who were healed had precisely a function of highlighting how futile this was: it was in fact a device to further the idea that Jesus' fame as a miracle worker spread far and wide.

What about the cases, however, where Jesus commands the demons to be silent because they know who he is? Here it should be noted that it is not the fact that Jesus is the Messiah that the demons reveal, but that he is the "Son of God," or the "Holy One of God." This has led at least one scholar to portray the secret as not so much a "messianic secret" but a secret around the identity of Jesus with God.[5] Other scholars note that the silencing of demons is part of what happens in an exorcism anyway.

The clearest instance where the messianic secret is operating is when Jesus tells the disciples not to say anything about who he is after Peter has explicitly identified him as the Messiah (8:29–30). Shortly thereafter, Jesus enjoins silence upon three of the disciples (Peter, James, and John) after they have witnessed his transfiguration (Mark 9:9). Jesus tells these disciples that they are not to say anything about what they have seen until after "the Son of Man [has]

5. Kingsbury, *Conflict in Mark*, 43–45, 57.

Who Is Jesus?

risen from the dead." Does this confirm Wrede's view that it is only after the resurrection that Jesus is recognized as the Messiah? A difficulty here is that the implied author does not present this as being the case. It seems that what Jesus says and does prior to his death is sufficient for the authorities, at least, to suspect that he is making a claim to be the Messiah. In the trial before the Jewish council, the high priest is represented as asking Jesus directly, "Are you the Messiah, the Son of the Blessed One?" To which Jesus gives the unequivocal reply, "I am" (14:61–62a). What makes this a difficulty for Wrede's thesis is that it indicates that the implied author did not consistently maintain the idea that before the resurrection Jesus kept claims to being the Messiah secret.

Indeed, Jesus himself raises the question of the Messiah in an interesting manner. While teaching in the temple, he asks this question: "How can the scribes say that the Messiah is the son of David?" (12:35). He then goes on to cite a scripture, one of the psalms traditionally attributed to David (Ps 110:1): "The Lord said to my Lord, 'Sit at my right hand, until I put your enemies under your feet.'" Jesus then asks: "David himself calls him Lord; so how can he be his son?" (12:37). There are a couple of intriguing issues to do with this question. First, it is not clear to whom the question is addressed. In the previous part of this chapter, Jesus has had to parry questions from his opponents, and a scribe who seems genuinely sincere in his question, and whom Jesus commends. After the exchange with the scribe, the narrator says that "after that no one dared to ask [Jesus] any question" (12:34b). But, it is not clear that Jesus' questions are directed at any of these interlocutors.

Nor do Jesus' questions receive a reply. The narrator simply tells the reader that "the large crowd was listening to him with delight" (12:37b). If we look at the original context of the psalm Jesus quotes, we might think that Jesus' questions are misconceived. We might assume that David intended the "lord" to whom the Lord God speaks in this psalm to refer to himself or to signify the king. Yet, here is Jesus referring the quotation to the Messiah: and he is using the quotation in such a way as to raise the question about the identity of the Messiah and the Messiah's "relationship" to David. If the Messiah cannot be David's son (as Jesus' question implies), whose son is he? Or, to phrase the question another way, if the conventional understanding of the Messiah as "Son of David" is not a wholly accurate way to understand him, what is the correct understanding?

Here, perhaps, is a clue to the "messianic secret." The implied author structures the narrative in such a way as to help the reader arrive at the correct understanding of what it means to call Jesus "the Messiah." Indeed, to return to the episode in Mark 8, when Peter makes his declaration, in answer to Jesus' question about whom they think he is, the next question that the implied author wants to explore is: What does it mean to call Jesus "Messiah"? What sort of Messiah is Jesus?

After Peter has said that Jesus is the Messiah (or, Christ), and Jesus has ordered the disciples to keep this quiet, Jesus goes on to speak about the fact that the "Son of Man"[6] must suffer, and face rejection by the Jewish authorities, be put to death, and rise again after three days. Jesus

---

6. "The Son of Man" is a term found only on the lips of Jesus in this Gospel (at Mark 9:9, the Greek might be translated either as direct speech or as reported speech of Jesus). As a "title," the term has been subjected to extensive discussion among scholars, including the question whether in Mark Jesus is referring to himself or someone else. I believe that the implied author associates the use of this descriptor with Jesus in such a way that it is certain that the reader is to understand that in using the term, Jesus is making a self-reference. See the comments by Broadhead, *Naming Jesus*, 131.

repeats this teaching twice more in the chapters that follow. The disciples struggle both to understand and to accept this teaching that defines what it means to be the Messiah. Indeed, the narrative develops in such a way as to suggest that they never truly do come to terms with this aspect of Jesus' identity: this is a theme we shall explore further in the next chapter. But it seems clear that, by the time the high priest asks Jesus the question of his identity in Mark 14:61, the contours of what it means to call Jesus "Messiah," and for him to call himself "Son of Man," have been sufficiently clearly laid out in the narrative, to enable the implied author to place a statement of "full disclosure" on Jesus' lips.

This full disclosure, however, comes in the context of a narrative that paints a picture of Jesus consisting of many colors. The reader must approach the question of who Jesus is with what has been imparted across the whole of the narrative in mind. So we must return to the prologue to explore some of the other descriptors used of Jesus. This not only will enable us to understand the identity of Jesus on the wide canvas of the story, but will put the question of the "messianic secret" in the perspective from which, I will suggest, the implied author wishes the reader to view it.

JESUS THE SON OF GOD

"The beginning of the good news of Jesus Christ, the Son of God" (Mark 1:1). It is possible that this striking beginning to the narrative did not include the words, "the Son of God." The manuscript evidence is mixed: the words are omitted in some important manuscripts, yet other manuscripts give strong support for their inclusion.[7] Many scholars accept that the original text did include the words.

7. The committee that decided on the text of the Greek for the Bible Society's edition of the Greek New Testament put the words in

Even if the words did not appear in the Gospel originally, it would be difficult for a reader to read this story without forming the understanding that the implied author identifies Jesus as God's Son. Within the prologue, a voice from heaven (without a doubt the voice of God) refers to Jesus as "my Son" (1:11). This heavenly affirmation is repeated later in the story, in the event known as "the Transfiguration," which includes a voice saying, "This is my Son, the Beloved: listen to him!" (9:7). One of those possessed of a demon shouts: "What have you to do with me, Jesus, Son of the Most High God?" (5:7). Even the high priest, at Jesus' trial, asks Jesus if he is "the Messiah, the Son of the Blessed One" ("Blessed One" being a circumlocution for God; 14:61). When the centurion who is in charge of Jesus' crucifixion sees how he dies, he is moved to say, "Truly this man was God's Son" (15:39).

That Jesus is to be associated in some way with God, perhaps even identified with God, is suggested by the implied author's citation of "Isaiah." Though the narrator states that the quotation is written in the prophet Isaiah, scholars recognize that the citation is actually a conflation of three texts: Isaiah 40:3, Exodus 23:20, and Malachi 3:1. The conflation of these texts has the effect of applying what referred in the original contexts to Israel (in the case of Exod 23:20), or Israel's God (Mal 3:1 and Isa 40:3) to Jesus, and to John the Baptist as the messenger. Thus the "Lord" whose way "the voice" (John) crying in the wilderness is to prepare is Jesus. This identification of Jesus as "the Lord" is suggested again in the story of the healing of the Gerasene demoniac (Mark 5:1–20) when, after he has been healed,

---

square brackets and gave the insertion of the words a "C" rating. This means that they were doubtful as to what the correct reading should be, but felt that it was not advisable to omit the words from the main text altogether; see Metzger, *Textual Commentary*, 62.

Who Is Jesus?

the demoniac pleads with Jesus to be allowed to accompany him. Jesus, however, sends him back to his home to tell his friends "how much the Lord has done for you, and what mercy he has shown to you." This could well mean that Jesus intends the man to tell everyone how much God has done for him, and that would cohere well with the implied author's intentions. However, the narrator informs the reader that the man goes away and proclaims how much *Jesus* had done for him. The conflation of the identity of Jesus with that of God is an ambiguity that the implied author does nothing to dispel.

There is, furthermore, the instance where Jesus himself appears to conflate the idea of the Messiah as "the Lord" with God as the Lord who invites him to sit at God's right hand. The NRSV captures this by capitalizing both instances of Lord: "The Lord said to my Lord" (12:36).[8] The question is what the implied author intends to mean by having the reader understand Jesus as "the Lord." Indeed, the question of what the implied author would have meant by calling Jesus "the Son of God" is much debated. This is a large question. However, a clearer understanding may only be gained by attending to what the narrative as a whole suggests. So we must continue our exploration of what emerges as we attend to the prologue of this story.

THE STRONGER ONE

In the prologue, in addition to the narrator's commentary (which includes the citation of scripture) that conveys much important information, both explicitly given and by

---

8. Note that on Mark 1:3, Adela Yarbro Collins says in a footnote: "See also Mark 12:36, where . . . both God and the Messiah (from the perspective of the author of Mark) are given the epithet 'Lord' [*kurios*]"; Collins, *Mark*, 137.

inference, about how Jesus is to be understood, characters also say things about Jesus that add color and complexity to the overall portrait. One of these is John the Baptist who is cast in the role of "the messenger" who is to prepare Jesus' way. John's proclamation about Jesus begins as follows: "The one who is more powerful than I is coming after me" (1:7a). The Greek might be translated "the Stronger One."

In what sense should Jesus be understood as the one stronger than John the Baptist? There is a clue in the respective roles of John and Jesus, and the way John is described. In Mark 1:14, the narrator says that after John has been put in prison, Jesus comes preaching the kingdom of God. Indeed, as the story makes clear, in the teaching and deeds of Jesus the kingdom of God is being brought about: it has come near. John the Baptist's role is to prepare the way for the announcement and inauguration of this kingdom. John's role as forerunner, and the one who prepares the way for the Messiah, is underlined by the way in which his dress is described. His wardrobe of a camel's hair tunic and leather belt reminds the reader of Elijah (described in 2 Kgs 1:8 as a hairy man with a leather belt around his waist). Indeed, the association of John with Elijah is implied by the logic of the story later when Jesus speaks of John as the "Elijah" who comes before "the Son of Man" (Mark 9:11–13). On the basis of Malachi 3:1, Elijah was expected to return before the "day of the Lord"; or, before the Messiah came.

There is a further association with an Old Testament character in the description of John's diet. He is said to eat locusts and wild honey. Many scholars see this as the typical diet of a desert dweller. But there is one character in the Old Testament who is specifically described as eating wild honey. This is Samson, who finds some wild honey in the carcass of a lion (described in his riddle as "the strong

Who Is Jesus?

one"[9]) that he has previously overpowered and killed (see Judg 14:5–9, 14). Given that immediately after this description of John's diet, one that evokes Samson's diet, John will speak of "the stronger one"; this seems to me to be highly suggestive.

Samson's strength was a physical prowess that enabled him to overpower a young lion, and also to gain victories over Israel's enemies, the Philistines. Jesus, whose ministry John introduces and describes as "the stronger one," demonstrates a power over the spiritual enemies of Israel: Satan, the adversary, and the evil spirits. His is not a physical prowess but a spiritual strength, and a large part of his activity in bringing the kingdom of God in Mark's story has to do with the overpowering of the forces of evil.

Indeed, the very first healing, the first action that Jesus performs after beginning his preaching of the kingdom and after he has called four disciples, is to perform an exorcism (1:21–28). As well as knowing who Jesus is, the evil spirits know that in Jesus they have met their match. They are represented as calling out such things as: "Have you come to destroy us?" (1:24); "What have you to do with me? . . . Do not torment me" (this from a man possessed by many spirits, who beg not to be utterly destroyed; see 5:7–10).

Early in the story (see Mark 3:20–27) there is a significant exchange between Jesus and some scribes from Jerusalem who accuse Jesus of being himself possessed by Beelzebul, and casting out demons by this "ruler of the demons." Jesus asks how Satan can cast out Satan, and draws an analogy with a kingdom (or "a house") that will not be able to continue to exist securely if it is divided against

---

9. Indeed, in Judg 14:14, the word in the Septuagint (the Greek translation of the Hebrew Bible or Christian Old Testament) used for "the strong" (Greek; *ischurou*) is the same as that used in Mark 1:7 for "the stronger one" (Greek: *ischuroteros*).

itself. In the course of the "parable" Jesus makes this significant statement: "But no one can enter a strong man's (Greek: *ischuterou*, the genitive form of *ischuros*[10]) house and plunder his property without first tying up the strong man; then indeed the house can be plundered" (v. 27). The implication is that Jesus is the one who is stronger (Greek: *ho ischuroteros*; "the stronger one," 1:7) than Satan who is able to plunder his "house," and who is laying waste to Satan's kingdom.

Immediately after his baptism by John, Jesus is "expelled" by the Spirit into the wilderness where he is tempted by Satan (1:12–13). Unlike the account of Jesus' temptation in the Gospels of Matthew and Luke, the account here is very terse. A significant feature of this brief mention of the temptation of Jesus by Satan is that nothing is said about Satan departing and leaving Jesus alone (as is the case in Matthew, see Matt 4:11; or in Luke, see Luke 4:13). This may suggest that for the implied author Jesus engages with Satan in a struggle that lasts throughout Jesus' ministry in Galilee, and that is finally resolved in the resurrection. The presence of wild beasts with Jesus in the wilderness (a puzzling and unexplained feature) may represent that Jesus is surrounded by danger and the forces of evil; ranged against the wild beasts are the angels who wait on Jesus. On the other hand, it may also represent the fact that in Jesus the kingdom of peace (when humans and wild animals will live together in harmony; see Isa 11:6–9; Hos 2:18) is coming into being. Whatever the case, Jesus is "the stronger one" who, in the power of the indwelling Spirit, confronts the forces of evil, the powers ranged against the kingdom of God, and overpowers them.

---

10. The grammatical form of this should be understood basically as a gerund: that is, a noun (or an "adjectival-noun") that has been formed from a verb or adverb.

Who Is Jesus?

THE BELOVED SON WHO RULES AS A SERVANT

The prologue describes the baptism of Jesus by John in the Jordan. After he has been baptized Jesus sees the heavens torn apart and the Spirit descends onto (or into) him. It is perhaps too much to say that God is a character in the story. Nevertheless, a voice (which is most certainly to be understood as the voice of God) makes a statement about Jesus. "You are my Son, the Beloved; with you I am well pleased" (1:11).

This statement is, in fact, another composite scriptural quotation. Examining the contexts of the scriptures from which the statement is drawn suggests another perspective from which the implied author wishes the reader to view Jesus. The first part of the statement is drawn from Psalm 2:7, which reads: "I will tell of the decree of the Lord: He said to me, 'You are my son; today I have begotten you.'" Psalm 2 is a "royal psalm" that speaks of the way in which God establishes and supports the king (his "anointed," Ps 2:2), especially in the face of opposition from the nations. This suggests that one way to see Jesus is as a "king": indeed as God's anointed king.

Indeed, the implied author makes something of this designation during Jesus' trial and crucifixion. Pilate, without any prior explanation of why he does so, asks Jesus point blank: "Are you the King of the Jews?" (15:2). The reader must assume that the charge that the chief priests, elders, scribes, and the whole council bring against Jesus, when they present him to Pilate, is that he claimed to be, or perhaps was acting as if he were, "the King of the Jews." Certainly, the narrator indicates that this is the charge upon which Jesus is condemned to be crucified (15:32). This charge has earlier enabled the Roman soldiers to make fun

37

of Jesus, as they prepare to crucify him, by dressing him up in "royal robes," crowning him with a crown of thorns, and pretending to pay homage to him as "the King of the Jews" (15:16–20).

As he hangs on the cross, the chief priests and the scribes, perhaps congratulating themselves that they have at last been able to rid themselves of this troublemaker, scornfully tell each other that this "Christ, the King of Israel" should now descend from the cross to convince them of his kingly position. In this mocking comment, there is perhaps a clue to the way in which "King of Israel" is to be understood. It is a designation for the Messiah, who was expected to come from the kingly line of David. In this sense, the Messiah could be understood as a "son" of David. One character in the Gospel story, a blind man called Bartimaeus, has actually used the descriptor "Son of David" in appealing to Jesus for healing (Mark 10:47–48). Jesus does not appear, on that occasion, to disown the description.

We have already seen that Jesus does not deny that he is the Messiah when he is asked by the high priest about his identity. It is a little difficult, however, to determine Jesus' attitude to the designation "the King of the Jews." When Pilate asks him if he is "the King of the Jews," Jesus' reply is enigmatic. He does not say, "I am," but "You say so." Is that an affirmation: to be understood as "You've said it"; and implying that Pilate has hit the nail on the head? Or is it an evasion: "Well, that's what you say"?

Whether Jesus affirms or refuses to endorse the designation "the King of the Jews" as appropriate to his identity, there is one story told when Jesus appears to be promoting the idea of kingship, and a messianic kingship at that. As Jesus approaches Jerusalem, nearing the end of his one fateful journey there, he sends two disciples ahead into a nearby village to find and bring to him a young colt. Jesus then sits

Who Is Jesus?

on this colt in order to make his entry to Jerusalem. Commentators note that to ride into Jerusalem is itself unusual if Jesus is going as a pilgrim to Jerusalem: the usual practice was to walk. Be that as it may, the effect of Jesus' action on the accompanying disciples and the crowd is interesting and electric. They spread their cloaks on the road before him, and some cut branches from nearby trees to spread, as well. The narrator informs the reader that "those who went ahead and those who followed were shouting, 'Hosanna! Blessed is the one who comes in the name of the Lord! Blessed is the coming kingdom of our ancestor David! Hosanna in highest heaven!'" (11:9–10).

What is happening here? The reaction of the disciples and the crowd suggest that they see this as the arrival of the messianic king, that expected descendent of David ("the Son of David") who would come "in the name of the Lord" to establish the messianic kingdom. Readers familiar with their Scriptures might recognize in Jesus' choice of conveyance an evocation of the king described in Zechariah 9:9. "Rejoice greatly, O daughter of Zion! Shout aloud, O daughter of Jerusalem! Lo, your king comes to you: triumphant and victorious is he, humble and riding on a donkey, on a colt, the foal of a donkey." It would appear that in his decision to ride into Jerusalem on a young donkey, Jesus is deliberately inviting people to associate him with the "king" who comes in triumph to establish the kingdom.

But what sort of a king is Jesus to be, and what nature of kingship will he adopt? Here the second part of the scriptural citation in Mark 1:11 is pertinent. The voice from heaven states that Jesus is "the Beloved; with you I am well pleased." The phrase "with you I am well pleased" evokes Isaiah 42:1, which reads: "Here is my servant, whom I uphold, my chosen, *in whom my soul delights*: I have put my spirit upon him; he will bring forth justice to the nations."

While the Greek does not exactly reproduce what is found in the Septuagint (it is closer to the Hebrew and may be a translation of that) the correspondence in thought is sufficiently strong to encourage most commentators to think that here the implied author has in mind the text from Isaiah. It is interesting that Isaiah 42:1 also states that God puts his spirit upon the servant and this provides a further correspondence with the baptism of Jesus as the Spirit is said to descend upon him just before the voice speaks.

This verse opens what is known as the first of the "Servant Songs," and is one of a complex of passages in Isaiah that speak of the one who would fulfill a special role as God's servant. It is very possible that in evoking this text, the implied author associates Jesus with the servant of Isaiah who would fulfill a redemptive role on behalf of Israel through suffering (see Isa 52:13—53:12, a text that was widely applied to Jesus by early Christians). The term "my beloved" might be a substitute for Isaiah's "my chosen"; but some commentators think it may evoke the way in which Abraham's son Isaac is referred to in the Septuagint as "your beloved son" in Genesis 22 (see Gen 22:2, 12, 16).[11] Thus, the implied author may also imply here that Jesus is like Isaac, a "beloved son" who is offered up as a sacrifice. As Frank Moloney says: "Perhaps this suggestion of the love between Abraham and Isaac, whom [Abraham] was asked to sacrifice as a sign of his unconditional allegiance to YHWH, is a first subtle hint of Jesus' destiny."[12]

When Jesus begins, in the latter part of the Gospel story, to teach his disciples what it means to be the Messiah in three patterned teaching sessions, he puts the emphasis ever more strongly on the fact that the "Son of Man"

---

11. The Septuagint (LXX) translates the Hebrew word *yahid* ("only," see NRSV) with *agapētos* ("beloved").

12. Moloney, *Gospel of Mark*, 37.

Who Is Jesus?

must suffer (see 8:31; 9:31; 10:33–34). In each case, as they have difficulty grasping the implications, Jesus provides further explanatory teaching. On the last occasion, having explained yet again the implications of his style of messiahship for discipleship, Jesus concludes with a significant statement. "For the Son of Man came," he says, "not to be served but to serve, and to give his life a ransom for many" (10:45).

By bringing together the two texts (Ps 2:7 and Isa 42:1), the implied author makes the point that Jesus is to be understood as a king, God's anointed. By the time his story was written, Psalm 2 was understood by many Jews as speaking about the Messiah: so that the idea of the Davidic Messiah is, perhaps, also in play. But the evocation of the Suffering Servant of Isaiah places this kingship in a new perspective. As the Messiah (and we may note that God's voice confirms what the narrator says in 1:1), Jesus will take up the role of a servant. His obedience to God will take him on a road that leads to death on a cross. If there is a coronation for this king, then it comes just before he is put on the cross: it is a "coronation" carried out by mocking soldiers who dress Jesus in a royal robe and force a crown of thorns down onto his brow (15:16–20). Though the chief priests and the scribes intend to mock, there is an ironic truth in their words: "He saved others; he cannot save himself. Let the Messiah, the King of Israel, come down from the cross now, so that we may see and believe" (15:31–32). What it means for Jesus to be a Messiah who cannot save himself is the burden of the implied author's narrative.

THE SON OF MAN AND THE "ONE LOAF"

I have been considering some of the images and descriptors of Jesus that are found in the prologue. To be sure, I have not confined our consideration of these to material found only in the prologue; for we must understand the presentation of Jesus in this Gospel as emerging from the story as a whole. This is an aspect I shall return to shortly. But first, I will discuss two more images, or descriptors, of Jesus that are found in this Gospel's story. One of these appears explicitly in the story: the other is an implicit image.

While the narrator, and the characters, use many images and descriptors to refer to Jesus' identity (Christ, Son of God, Holy One of God, Son of David, a prophet, Elijah, John the Baptist, teacher, rabbi, "lord"[13]), Jesus consistently uses one of himself: Son of Man. My assertion here is not uncontroversial. There are some scholars (and perhaps other readers) who consider that Jesus refers to a figure other than himself when he uses this term. However, I believe that the contexts and the manner in which Jesus' use of the descriptor "Son of Man" appear in the story make this almost certainly a term of self-description. Indeed, not to take "Son of Man" as referring to Jesus would, in some instances, be counter-intuitive. It would make it difficult to make sense of the story.

There are a couple of observations to be made about Jesus' use of this descriptor. First, all but two of the instances where "Son of Man" appear are found in the second part of the story. That is, they appear after Peter has identified Jesus as "the Christ" and as Jesus begins to explain what it means to understand his role as "the Christ." Second, Jesus uses this self-appellation when he is talking of the future: here

---

13. Some who observe what Jesus says and does think that he is John the Baptist returned to life; King Herod most certainly believes this (see, e.g., Mark 6:14–16). "Lord" (Greek: *kurios*) might simply be a term of respect, and "Sir" might be an appropriate alternative translation. However, occasionally the implied author chooses to make both its use and its referent ambiguous (see, e.g., Mark 1:3; 5:19; 11:3).

Who Is Jesus?

the future events in view are of two kinds. One complex of events will find its fulfillment within the world and time of the story: Jesus speaks of himself as "Son of Man" when he is teaching the disciples about his own immediate future when he will be subject to torture and rejection by the Jewish authorities, when he will suffer death and then rise again (8:31; 9:31; 10:33–34; cf. also 14:21, 41). As the reported command to the three disciples, as they descend from the Mount of Transfiguration, places an embargo on speaking about what they had seen "until after the Son of Man had risen from the dead" (9:9), I think that this instance can be included in this first set of future-oriented statements.

Other "Son of Man" references have in view a complex of future events (perhaps, an event?) that will occur at some indeterminate time when "the Son of Man . . . comes in the glory of his Father with the holy angels" (9:38, see also 13:26; 14:62). It is interesting, I think, that in the two places where Jesus is most explicitly identified as "the Messiah," Jesus uses the self-designation "Son of Man." In the first instance, when Peter identifies Jesus as "the Messiah" (8:29), Jesus immediately begins to teach the disciples about his suffering, death, and resurrection; in other words, the focus is on the "near future." In the other instance, when the high priest asks Jesus whether he is the Messiah, Jesus replies in the affirmative and immediately speaks about the future coming of the Son of Man (14:61–62): the focus here is on the "indeterminate future."

In passing we might note that the two instances when Jesus refers to himself as the Son of Man early in the story are both occasions when he is making a claim to an unusual authority: in the first instance an authority to forgive sins (2:10), and in the second instance, an authority over the Sabbath, an authority to determine what is allowable as Sabbath activity (2:27). But what did Jesus mean when he referred to himself as the "Son of Man"? Scholars have debated both the meaning of the term "Son of Man" and Jesus' use of it in reference to himself for decades and exhaustively. Some would maintain that it can be understood as another way of saying "I": in other words, it means "a human like myself," or "a man like me"; or some cases it might simply mean "a human being." It is possible, for instance, that in the case of Jesus' saying about the Sabbath, it might simply be understood to mean that the Sabbath is intended to benefit humans, and not the other way around. Thus, a human being is lord (or, master) even of the Sabbath.

It is possible that the implied author, when he has Jesus use the term "Son of Man" of himself, is simply intending it to be a circumlocution for "I."[14] However, as we have seen, in the first two instances Jesus is using it in a manner that also implies some form of authority. Also, the narrative shows quite clearly that Jesus is capable of using the simple first person pronoun to refer to himself. An analysis of the instances where the term is most often used shows that Jesus is speaking about the future (near or indeterminate) and is making some sort of point about his identity. He appears to be using the term as his own preferred descriptor for his identity and role as one who is about the business of bringing in God's kingdom.

Many scholars note that one source for this descriptor may well be the description in Daniel 7:13–14 of one "like a human being," or, to translate the Greek of the Septuagint more literally, "like a son of man" (RSV). It suggests that this one who is "like a son of man" will receive the power to

14. It should be noted that the term "Son of Man" always appears in the Gospel as a descriptor that Jesus uses of himself, except where the narrator is providing reported speech of Jesus, as for example in Mark 8:31 (possibly) and 9:9 (probably), and is not used by the narrator, or other characters, of Jesus. This has led scholars to assume that this is a manner of speech that goes back to the historical Jesus.

Who Is Jesus?

rule from God ("the Ancient of Days"). By the time of the first century this Danielic image probably gave rise to the idea of an apocalyptic figure who would help to establish the kingdom of God. It is likely that the idea of a heavenly "Son of Man" was associated with the Messiah.[15] Whatever background associations may have been available to the original readers, it is clear that the implied author used the descriptor to flesh out the implied readers understanding of Jesus as the Messiah in two main ways.

Jesus, as the "Son of Man," was to come at some indeterminate time in the future to establish God's reign. As "Son of Man," like the "Son of Man" in Daniel, he would come with all the authority and power of God (represented in Jesus' words to the high priest by the fact that the Son of Man would be "seated at the right hand of the Power"; Mark 14:62). In the world of the story, this is a picture of the "Son of Man" that would be quite acceptable and understood by Jesus' disciples. Of course the Son of Man (that is, the Messiah) would come "with great glory" and would have God's authority to establish his kingly rule. When that happened, the disciples expected to share in that "glory": an issue that was of interest to them was what the pecking order would be within that kingdom.

What the disciples found difficult to grasp was the teaching of Jesus that the "Son of Man" would be subject to suffering, and to rejection by the authorities. It was disconcerting and disturbing to them that Jesus would speak of a future that would see the humiliation and death of the "Son of Man." They were quite unable to understand what Jesus'

15. The question of what the messianic expectations were at the time the Gospel of Mark was written is a much-debated issue, let alone what might have been understood in wider Jewish literature and society by the term, "Son of Man." On "Son of Man," see Broadhead, *Naming Jesus*, ch. 13. A brief, useful summary on the term may also be found in Boring, *Mark*, 251–52.

reference to the resurrection of the "Son of Man," after three days, could mean. The device by which the implied author shows Jesus teaching the disciples about the "Son of Man" who would suffer, and the continued inability of the disciples to understand this teaching, is the implied author's way of redefining and reorienting the nature of Jesus' messiahship for the implied reader. This type of Messiah brought about the kingdom of God by walking a path of suffering and death. The crucifixion of Jesus was not a mistake. It was a necessity.

Why the death of Jesus was fundamental to Jesus' messiahship is brought out in the Gospel story by an implicit image of Jesus as "the one loaf." The story includes two occasions on which Jesus feeds large crowds on the basis of a small ration of bread: on one occasion, five thousand are fed from fives loaves (Mark 6:30–44), and on the other, four thousand are fed from seven loaves (Mark 8:1–10). Shortly after the second occasion, the narrator tells a story of the disciples and Jesus taking a boat trip during which Jesus brings up the subject of the "yeast" of the Pharisees and of Herod (Mark 8:14–21). The narrator prefaces this discussion by informing the reader that the disciples had forgotten to bring any bread: rather, that they had only one loaf with them in the boat. They think that Jesus' words about yeast is a subtle way of admonishing them for their poor provisioning. Jesus reminds them about the two feeding miracles: asking them how much bread had been left over in each case. When they reply that in the case of the feeding of the five thousand, there had been twelve baskets of leftovers, and in the case of the four thousand there had been seven baskets of leftovers, Jesus asks: "Do you not yet understand?"

No answer is given to Jesus' question. The question might be one that the implied reader does not know how to

Who Is Jesus?

answer either.[16] What are the disciples to understand? That on account of the feeding miracles, the disciples should know by now that one loaf is more than sufficient? By this stage in the story, however, the implied reader may well suspect that "bread" and "loaves" are a symbol of something else. For one thing, in this very story, Jesus asks questions of the disciples that remind the implied reader of an earlier exchange when Jesus has spoken about "the secret of the kingdom." The questions Jesus asks are these (prompted by the disciples concern about having no bread): "Why are you talking about having no bread? Do you still not perceive or understand? Do you have eyes, and fail to see? Do you have ears, and fail to hear?" (8:17–18).

To have eyes that do not see and ears that cannot hear, and to fail to be able to perceive or understand, are conditions which pertain to "those outside," that is, those to whom the "secret of the kingdom" has not been given. The disciples, however, have been given the secret: there is no question in Jesus' mind that they are on "the inside" and are privy to this "secret" (see Mark 4:10–12). But what is this "secret": what should the disciples be able to perceive and understand? Can it have anything to do with understanding the identity of Jesus?

Indeed, it very well might. An incident which occurs directly after the first feeding miracle, and where the narrator refers to "loaves," makes this likely (Mark 6:45–52). Jesus, after the feeding of the five thousand, has dispatched the disciples in a boat by themselves. He remains behind to pray while they head off for Bethsaida on the other side

---

16. The implied reader is the "reader" evoked by the narrative itself, who responds to the cues (and clues) implanted in the text by the implied author. In this case, I suggest, the implied reader is prompted by the unanswered question to assess the level of the disciples' understanding.

of the lake. They run into difficulties: they are rowing into a very strong headwind. Jesus appears, walking on the sea, and making as if to pass they by. They are terrified, believing that they are seeing a ghost. Immediately, Jesus reassures them: "Take heart, it is I: do not be afraid" (the phrase, "it is I," may well remind the implied reader of the words of God to Moses at the burning bush). Jesus gets into the boat with them, and the wind ceases. The disciples are, naturally enough, "utterly astounded." The narrator then concludes the story with an enigmatic statement: "for they did not understand about the loaves, but their hearts were hardened."

How should understanding about the loaves enable them to understand what has happened on the lake? Perhaps this is a piece of shorthand on the part of the implied author to make the point that the disciples do not understand what the feeding of the five thousand should convey about the identity of Jesus. Hardness of heart is a condition that afflicts those who do not understand the secret of the kingdom. Might the secret have something to do with what the disciples should understand about Jesus after he has met them on the lake and made the wind to cease?

Directly after the second feeding miracle, and before Jesus and the disciples embark on the boat trip where the issue of "yeast" and "one loaf / no bread" comes up, the narrator reports that Pharisees come and argue with Jesus, and ask for a sign from heaven. The account is terse, and there is no explanation as to what they are arguing about, or what the Pharisees want the sign to indicate. But the effect of their request is to make Jesus sigh deeply and say: "Why does this generation ask for a sign? Truly I tell you, no sign will be given to this generation?" The reader may well assume that the "sign" that the Pharisees desire has something to do with the basis of Jesus authority, or the nature of his identity. In that case, the reader may well detect an irony in

Who Is Jesus?

the placement of this request (or test) at this point in the narrative. Have there not been several "signs from heaven"? Has the feeding of the four thousand not provided yet one more?

If the theme of "bread" and "loaves" that has run through this section has something to do with what might be perceived and understood about the nature and identity of Jesus, then the reader might well discover another irony in the fact that the disciples have "one loaf" with them in the boat. As Christian readers they may well have detected echoes of eucharistic practice in the fact that at the feeding of the five thousand Jesus looks to heaven and blesses the bread before breaking it (6:41) and at the feeding of the four thousand Jesus gives thanks before breaking the bread (8:6). In the Greek, the word for giving thanks (*eucharistēsas*) is the word from which we get our English word "Eucharist" and was early on a traditional way of designating "the Lord's supper."[17]

Be that as it may, the reader will discover that when the narrator tells the story of the "last supper" prior to Jesus' death, he recounts how Jesus takes a loaf, we might say "one loaf," blesses it, breaks it, and distributes it to the disciples saying: "Take; this is my body." He follows this by distributing a cup of wine that represents his "blood of the new covenant." Hence, bread and wine comes to be symbolic

---

17. The name "Eucharist" was first applied to the commemoration of Jesus' death in the *Didache* (see *Didache* 9:1). Some scholars date this work toward the end of the first century, and it is possible that some of the material found in it witnesses to traditions contemporaneous with the New Testament writings. We cannot be sure, however, that the readers of Mark's Gospel were familiar with this name. Paul's reference to the institution of the Lord's Supper in 1 Cor 11:23–26 mentions that Jesus "gave thanks" (v. 24). It would seem that Paul is citing a tradition as his account bears a strong resemblance to the accounts as found in the Synoptic Gospels. It is likely that the ancient name, Eucharist, arose because of these accounts.

of the death of Jesus on behalf of "many." When, earlier in the story, the disciples set out on their journey with only "one loaf," they little realize that with the presence of Jesus aboard they have all the "bread" they need. On a second reading, the reader might consider the irony that symbolically, the "one loaf" the disciples have with them is the one who will give his "body" (symbolized in a loaf of bread) on their behalf.[18]

MARK'S STORY OF JESUS AND THE QUESTION OF JESUS' IDENTITY

So far I have been looking at the way in which the implied author raises the question of Jesus' identity by exploring some of the images and descriptors (or what scholars often call "titles") that the implied author uses of Jesus.[19] It is important to remember that the implied author casts the

---

18. There is no certainty that the evangelist who wrote the Gospel of John knew Mark's Gospel, though scholars debate this possibility. Sometimes I find myself musing on the possibility that he did; and that his Gospel is, as it were, the first "commentary," or an early reader's response to the Gospel of Mark. Certainly, his discourse on Jesus as "the bread of life" following his account of the feeding of the five thousand (John 6) almost seems to pick up the kind of reading of Mark's Gospel that I am suggesting here.

19. I would prefer not to use the term "titles" as this may suggest that the implied author is drawing upon a set of commonly or widely understood and used descriptions for Jesus available within the Christian tradition, and arising out of interaction with a broader background of understanding and use within Jewish and Greco-Roman thought and literature. To a degree, this may well be the case: and those interested may follow the scholarly discussion of this in the literature on the Gospel. But, in the first analysis, it is better to try and understand how the implied author uses these descriptors within the Gospel story itself, and what this usage contributes to the picture of Jesus that emerges there.

Who Is Jesus?

question of Jesus' identity in the form of a story. This carries a couple of important implications for the way in which this identity is formed and accessed by the implied reader that I shall discuss briefly here. Much more than I shall say here might be written: but that would require another book. What I hope this discussion might do is alert you to these issues so that they can inform your own approach to a reading of this story.

The first implication of casting the identity of Jesus into the form of a story is that the picture of Jesus that emerges is one that is gained in a cumulative manner, and is comprehensive and coherent. By this I mean that everything that Jesus is represented as saying and doing, and all the descriptors that are applied to Jesus by the narrator and the characters, and all their reactions and responses to Jesus combine to create the implied reader's (and actual readers, or hearers) grasp of who Jesus is. This means, for instance, that one part of the story will interact with and illuminate another part of the story. It also means that because it is a narrative, the understanding of Jesus gained is formed not only by the profile of the implied reader that emerges, but also by the way in which each real reader may negotiate the gaps and implicit features of the narrative differently. The understanding of Jesus' identity is informed by the reader as much as it is directed by the implied author's narrative strategy.

On a first reading of the story, an understanding of Jesus' identity will be achieved by being sequentially developed. In other words, more and more will be revealed to the reader as the story progresses: and readers will revise and enlarge their understanding of Jesus in the light of what they discover as they read, and in the light of the whole story. We shall see shortly that the implied author uses the sequential nature of narrative as part of his strategy to raise questions about the identity of Jesus in the mind of the reader.

A sequential reading, for example, reveals the nature of Jesus' authority and fills out for the reader what is meant when the narrator say that Jesus "taught as one having authority, and not as the scribes" (1:22). The exorcism which follows demonstrates that this authority enables Jesus to command unclean spirits, and they are obliged to obey him. This authority is reinforced by a massive exorcism in the region of Gerasa (5:1–20). Not only this, but Jesus' authority evidently includes the authority to forgive sins: demonstrated when Jesus tells a paralyzed man that his sins are forgiven, and when challenged, shows that he has that authority by also healing the man of his paralysis (2:1–12). Jesus abrogates to himself authority over the Sabbath, claiming an authority that redefines what is lawful and permissible, in the face of what the Pharisees and religious leaders would claim to be the conventional (and, no doubt, scripturally based) parameters of lawful Sabbath observance. His claim that the "Son of Man" is lord of the Sabbath (2:27) is immediately sustained by his freely choosing to heal a man's withered hand on the Sabbath (3:1–5). Here he demonstrates that life-giving activity is seen in concern for human well-being against a formal adherence to Sabbath regulations.

The authority that Jesus has to bring about human well-being in the face of human regulation is shown to extend even to those realms where human regulation cannot stretch, and where (his audience would presume) only God's authority holds sway. So Jesus proves to have authority to still the forces of nature (4:35–41), and even to restore the dead to life (5:35–43). Some characters have already assumed that Jesus is trespassing on God's authority when he pronounces the forgiveness of the paralytic's sins (2:7).

Who Is Jesus?

The Greek construction can be understood to mean that Jesus is assuring the paralytic of the fact that God forgives him his sins. However, the fact that the critical scribes correctly understand what Jesus intends is shown when Jesus demonstrates that the "Son of Man has authority on earth to forgive sins" by healing the man of his paralysis.

Thus, a sequential reading of the story accumulates evidence that shows the implied reader that Jesus' authority is of a more-than-human sort, and throws into sharp relief the question of his identity in relation to God. When, toward the end of the story, the one human character not possessed of a demon is moved to say, "Truly this man was God's Son" (15:39), the implied reader is in a position to recognize the deep truth of Jesus' divine identity that this statement reinforces, even if ironically.[20]

A second or subsequent reading of the story will be informed by knowledge of the whole story which will throw fresh light on early stories, or fill out in greater color and depth of meaning the information imparted in, say, the prologue. I trust you will have caught something of the flavor of this as I made reference to later material when discussing the images and descriptors that emerge in the prologue. Even a first sequential reading will entail revisions and enlargement of understanding as fresh information is integrated into that previously acquired. As you read

---

20. Some readers, along with some commentators, may see in the centurion's words one final and further mocking statement. In other words, rather than being a perception of Jesus' true identity on the part of the centurion, the statement is meant to be taken as said sarcastically, "Well, so much for this 'Son of God'!" It is entirely possible to read the story this way: this simply reinforces my point that, as a narrative, the story is capable of being read in more than one way. It is difficult to think, however, that the implied reader would not consider the centurion's mocking statement as also ironically true, given the perspective on Jesus supplied by the implied author.

(or reread) the Gospel, reflect upon your own experience of reading it and see how far you agree.

A second implication of the Gospel's narrative form is that the story is told and structured in such a way as to make an impact on the reader or hearer. Thus the plot develops in a way that impacts the reader's reception and understanding of it. The implied author structures the sequence of the narrative in order to create an effect upon the implied reader. There are some widely recognized techniques in the story: one is the way in which the implied author creates a "sandwich" effect by embedding one story within another so that each interacts with the other providing a commentary upon one or both. Another technique is that of repetition that reinforces a point, or develops a theme (or themes). Yet another technique occurs where the implied author raises questions that remain unanswered. These techniques serve to develop aspects of the story beyond simply that of revealing the identity of Jesus, and I shall draw out some of these other aspects later in this book.

Two examples of the "sandwich" effect serve to undergird an understanding of Jesus' identity, along with other functions they may fulfill. One example is found in Mark 5 where Jesus is asked to go to the house of the leader of a synagogue, whose name is Jairus, as his daughter is lying ill and at the point of death. Jesus sets off for Jairus's home with him. However, their progress to Jairus's place is delayed by a woman who seeks healing from Jesus by surreptitiously approaching him in the crowd, from behind, and touching his cloak. In terms of the narrative, this interruption is effected by embedding the story of the woman's healing within the story of Jairus and his daughter. The insertion of this story has the effect of heightening the suspense as to whether Jesus will arrive at Jairus's home in time to heal his daughter. Indeed, when the story of Jairus resumes, the

Who Is Jesus?

reader discovers that the delay has meant that the daughter dies before Jesus arrives at the house. That Jesus still proceeds to the house and effects a restoration of the little girl to life raises even more sharply for the reader the nature of his identity.

Another example is found after Jesus' triumphal entry into Jerusalem. On the following day, as Jesus heads into Jerusalem, he goes to a fig tree to see if he can find figs on it. It is not the season for figs: but Jesus, finding no fruit on the tree curses it, and says, "May no one ever eat fruit from you again" (11:14). Jesus proceeds into Jerusalem, and drives out the merchants and money changers from the temple precincts, and prevents people from carrying goods through the temple. The following day, as Jesus and the disciples pass by the fig tree, Peter notices that the fig tree has withered. It is commonly recognized that the story of the cursing of the fig tree, enveloping as it does Jesus' action in the temple, provides a "parable" of the state of the temple: all show and no real "spiritual fruit." It is no longer a house of prayer for all the nations, but rather a den of robbers (11:17). In this case, it provides a rationale for Jesus' actions, which are largely unexplained.

But those readers who know their Scriptures may recall that the Lord (or the Messiah) was expected to come suddenly in judgment to "his house." Malachi 3:1 reads: "See, I am sending my messenger to prepare the way before me, and the Lord whom you seek will suddenly come to his temple." Indeed, the narrator had earlier alluded to this text in speaking of the coming of John the Baptist (1:2). Malachi 5:1 speaks of the Lord "drawing near" for judgment; and the accusation against Israel is that they are "robbing God" (Mal 3:8). Moreover, a number of texts in the Old Testament likened Israel to a fig tree that bore no figs, and thus came under judgment (see Jer 8:13; Hos 9:10, 16–17; Joel

1:7; Mic 7:1).[21] Finally, on "the day of the Lord," according to Zechariah 14:21, there would "no longer be traders in the house of the Lord of hosts."

It is impossible to know whether the implied author had a cluster of texts such as these in mind as he crafted the "fig tree parable" and the story of Jesus' action in the temple. Possibly, the fact that Jesus does not enact his demonstration on the day of his triumphal entry, but leaves it until the next day, is meant to evoke the fact that he "suddenly" comes to the temple in judgment (as underlined by the cursing of the fig tree). However, Jesus' reply to Peter, when the latter remarks upon the withered fig tree, turns the meaning of the action toward another end. Jesus turns his action in regards of the fig tree into a parable on the need for prayer and trust in the power of God. This possibly prepares the implied reader to understand that had Jesus chosen to tell the authorities by what authority he was doing "these things" (namely, cleansing the temple), he would have said: "On the authority and by the power of God."

Repetition is found in the doubling of the feeding miracle: five thousand fed in Mark 6:30–44 and four thousand in Mark 8:1–9. These two incidents are full of detail that suggest to readers a number of things about Jesus' preaching ministry, one of which is to underline the fact that he reaches out to both Jews and Gentiles. But, the doubling

---

21. A number of phrases, and ideas, in these texts are very suggestive for Mark's "fig tree parable." Jer 8:13 reads: "When I wanted to gather them [i.e., the people, or 'Israel'], says the Lord, there are no grapes on the vine, nor figs on the fig tree; even the leaves are withered, and what I gave them has passed away from them." Hos 9:10, 16–17, speaks of the fact that Israel was originally "like the first fruit on the fig tree, in its first season," but now was dried up at the root and unable to bear fruit. Mic 7:1 laments that he has become like one unable to find a "first-ripe fig for which I hunger" because "the faithful have disappeared from the land."

Who Is Jesus?

also reinforces for the implied reader, if not for the disciples, that Jesus is one who is able to supply the needs of many out of seemingly meager resources. The doubling also has the effect of increasing the sense of the disciples' slowness in learning to understand who Jesus is (a theme I shall take up in the next chapter).

Finally, we note the technique where the implied author sets up a series of questions for which no answer is received in the story. This, I suggest, has the effect of drawing the implied reader into the story to consider what this means. Generally, these unanswered questions raise doubts about the ability of the disciples to understand who Jesus is, or what the significance of his actions is. I have already alluded to the question that concludes the discussion about "yeast" and the "one loaf." Jesus' question "Do you not yet understand?" suggests to the implied reader that the disciples indeed do not yet understand. When and how they will come to understand is, at this point in the story, an open question. Readers may also feel somewhat uncertain about their own understanding.

Earlier in the story, Jesus and the disciples have been caught in a storm on Lake Galilee. When the disciples, fearful for their lives, have appealed to Jesus to save them, he has responded by ordering (the verb is "rebuke"—the same word used of Jesus' commands to the evil spirits) the wind to cease. It does so, and there is a "great calm." Then the narrator makes a significant statement: the disciples are filled with a great awe. Indeed, the Greek says that they "feared with a great fear" (if they were afraid before the great calm, they are even more afraid now!). And they say to one another: "Who then is this, that even the wind and the sea obey him?"

Who indeed? Again, the question sits there in the story, while the narrative moves on. A reader might be reminded of Psalm 107:23–32 (which speaks of the power of God over the wind and the sea—both to cause a storm and make it still), in particular verses 28–29: "Then they cried to the Lord in their trouble, and he brought them out from their distress; he made the storm be still, and the waves of the sea were hushed." Might the implied reader not find the answer to the question "Who is this?" here (reinforced as it is by the story of Jesus told in the Gospel as a whole)?

As I indicated in the first chapter, the implied author's surprising ending to the Gospel also functions to throw up a question. As the women run away from the tomb, saying nothing to anyone, a question hangs in the air: "Who can this Jesus of Nazareth be if the tomb cannot hold him, and if he has, as the young man has said, risen from the dead?"

3

Following Jesus on the Way

John the Baptist is represented as one who has come to "prepare the way of the Lord" (1:3). The Lord whose way John has come to prepare is Jesus.[1] After Jesus has been baptized, and has spent some time in the wilderness being tempted by Satan, and after John is arrested, Jesus makes his way to Galilee. There he begins to proclaim "the good news of God," and the implied author provides a summary of his preaching (1:15).

The first thing that Jesus does as he begins his teaching, preaching, and healing in Galilee is to call four fishermen to follow him (1:16–20). A major theme of Mark's Gospel is that of discipleship: what it means to be a follower

---

1. The reference could be to God, but the inference seems to be that this is to refer to Jesus, whose story this is, and of whom John is the precursor. Note that the previous verse speaks of a messenger who is coming to prepare "your way" (see the NRSV). The "you" is Jesus.

of Jesus. In this chapter we shall explore this theme, and the way in which the implied author develops it. However, before we do, it is important to notice a number of features of the plotting of the story, or the way in which the story is told, as it has a bearing upon the way in which we as readers receive this story.

THE STRUCTURE OF THE GOSPEL'S PLOT

The Gospel of Mark divides the ministry of Jesus into two periods. After the prologue (Mark 1:1–13),[2] Jesus is depicted as travelling about Galilee (and into some regions outside of Galilee) where he teaches and performs miracles of healing and exorcisms. At the midpoint of the story Jesus and his disciples head for the villages around Caesarea Philippi (Mark 8:27) where Jesus asks them a couple of significant questions about his identity and how he is perceived. Peter identifies Jesus as "the Christ" and from this point onward Jesus begins to teach the disciples what it means to be "the Christ," and what is involved in being a disciple of the Christ.

Although Jesus and his disciples continue in Galilee for a period (they are depicted as going to Capernaum in Mark 9:33), the focus of the story begins to fall upon the fate that awaits Jesus. He begins a journey toward Jerusalem (the one occasion in this Gospel when he travels there) where eventually he will be crucified. We might say that the "itinerary" of the Gospel goes like this. Jesus goes from Nazareth in Galilee to John at the Jordan, somewhere in the Judean wilderness. Upon his return to Galilee, Jesus, with his disciples, moves about making several trips across Lake

2. Some would include 1:14–15 as part of the prologue. In this case, the calling of the four disciples would be Jesus' first activity on arriving in Galilee.

Following Jesus on the Way

Galilee, and three side trips out of Galilee. One of these side trips is to the region of Gerasenes and the Decapolis (Mark 5:1–20). The next is into the territory of Tyre and Sidon, to the north of Galilee (this tour concludes with a return trip, via Lake Galilee, to the Decapolis). The third is up into the region around Caesarea Philippi (again to the north of Galilee). Finally, Jesus travels to Jerusalem, where he meets his death. This means that the journey to Jerusalem takes on a climatic significance in the Gospel's plot.

In addition to the overall structure of the plot, the implied author uses a number of plot devices and literary "tricks" that help to add depth and weight to various incidents and features of the developing plot. Two of these are the widely recognized "sandwich effect" and the tendency to repeat incidents or features of the plot. As noted in the previous chapter, the "sandwich effect" occurs when the implied author begins one story, then inserts another story into that story before concluding the first; or, to put it another way, a story is enveloped within another. The effect of this is to play features of one story off against the other and to make the two stories act as commentaries upon each other. An example occurs in Mark 6, where Jesus dispatches his disciples on a mission where they do many of the things that Jesus has accomplished in his mission. The story of John the Baptist's death, which is inserted between the sending out of Jesus' disciples and their return, serves to slow the story down so that the reader may assume that some time passes while the disciples undertake their mission. But, as the account of John's death arises because King Herod has heard of Jesus' fame, the incident also serves as a comparison between Jesus' and the disciples' currently successful mission and the fate of John the Baptist. As Jesus' mission has followed on from John's (1:14), this story may raise a question over the possible fate of Jesus. In addition, the note about John's disciples coming to bury John's body provides a counterpoint to the actions of Jesus' disciples after his death.

Repetitions are used at several points throughout the plot, and often serve to advance some theme or motif. For example, in Mark 4:35—8:21, there are three accounts of trips across Lake Galilee in a boat; and two accounts of large crowds being fed by Jesus using few rations. Two of the boat trips (the second and third) follow immediately upon each of the feeding stories.[3] We will see shortly how this repeating pattern of feeding stories followed by boat trips serves to unfold a theme of the disciples' progress in their understanding of who Jesus is and what it means to follow him. In Mark 8:2—10:45, Jesus engages the disciples in three "teaching sessions" when he explains to them what is to happen to him only to have them misunderstand him. Their subsequent activity demonstrates that they misunderstand the nature of his messiahship and do not grasp the meaning of discipleship. Each time Jesus attempts to bring understanding through further teaching intended to clarify the nature of discipleship. What is more, this section of the Gospel is sandwiched between two stories of the healing of a blind man. These stories act as "bookends" (or function as inclusios) to this section, and provide a commentary on the success, or otherwise, of the disciples' progress in understanding.

In addition, the implied author works with a number of images and motifs, some of them generated by the plot devices outlined above, that illuminate both what it means for Jesus to be the Christ, and the nature of discipleship. Hence, we will explore how these devices operate to enrich and develop the theme of discipleship.

3. In fact, the "third" boat trip is actually two trips taken in quick succession, see Mark 8:10, 13.

"THEY . . . FOLLOWED HIM": HOW THE IMPLIED AUTHOR VIEWS THE DISCIPLES

When Jesus calls the four fishermen, they are depicted as following him immediately. Simon and Andrew leave their nets, one of which they had been in the act of casting into the sea, and follow Jesus. James and John, mending their nets, leave their father Zebedee and those he has contracted in to help: it would seem that they leave behind a small fishing business. They are called to "follow Jesus" on the way; and so they do.

Soon after, Jesus sees a tax collector named Levi sitting at his tax booth. Jesus tells Levi to follow him, and like the four fisherman, Levi immediately abandons what he has been engaged in and follows Jesus. A feature of discipleship, as the implied author depicts it, is to be prepared to abandon everything for the sake of following Jesus. As an aside, it is probably the case that rather than abandoning everything completely, they are to put their skills and resources to new purposes, those of the kingdom of God. "Follow me and I will make you fish for people," Jesus tells Simon and Andrew. Their skills will be used not to catch fish, but to "catch" people. Later in the Gospel, Jesus makes use of a boat (see 4:1, 36; 5:21), and it is likely this belonged to one or other of the pairs of fishermen brothers. Immediately after Jesus has called Levi, the narrator states that Jesus uses Levi's house as a base for eating with other tax collectors and "sinners" (2:15–17). It is part of the purpose of Jesus' mission to "call" such people.

In contrast to these disciples, Jesus will be accosted by a wealthy man who asks what he must do to inherit eternal life (10:17–22). The upshot of the man's interchange with Jesus is that he is told to sell what he owns and give the money to the poor: his resources, in other words, are to be put to other purposes than for his own gratification. He is then to follow Jesus. The man finds that this is too demanding and turns away sorrowfully. Following a brief discussion about the difficulty that those who have wealth have in entering the kingdom of God, Peter is prompted to point out that they have left everything to follow Jesus.

The disciples are to be with Jesus, to listen to and to learn from him (the root meaning of the Greek word for "disciple" is "learner"). They are also to engage in proclaiming the message, and sharing Jesus' authority to "cast out demons" (3:15). The narrator describes Jesus as picking out twelve to be "sent out" for this purpose (3:13–19), and, in fact, such a mission is later described (see 6:6b–13), and their efforts are not without success, as they are able to cast out many demons, and anoint with oil many who are sick.

Initially, then, the disciples are portrayed in a positive light. They fulfill the requirements of disciples: they hear Jesus' call and they follow. They are able to share with Jesus in the mission of proclaiming the good news, exorcising and healing. Furthermore, they are portrayed as being Jesus' new "family" and as "insiders" who have been given "the secret of the kingdom of God." As we examine how the implied author conveys this to the reader, it is worth noting that the implied author also presents the possibility, the invitation, and the challenge of discipleship as open to everyone, not simply a select band of identified disciples. We shall see how this is conveyed momentarily, but already, at the meal following the call of Levi, the narrator has indicated that "there were many who followed him." It is not clear whether this refers to the fact that many tax collectors and sinners were following Jesus, or whether, already by this stage in the story, Jesus had many disciples.

Jesus' natural family come to restrain Jesus, for people are saying that he is out of his mind. They are described by

Following Jesus on the Way

the narrator as standing outside the house where Jesus is. In a reverse action ascribed to Jesus who calls and sends disciples, his family send messengers to him to call him. This action by the family is confirmed by a crowd sitting around Jesus who says to him, "Your mother and your brothers and sisters are outside, asking for you" (3:32). Jesus responds by asking, "Who are my mother and my brothers?" The narrator then states that he looks at those who sat around him and continues, "Here are my mother and my brothers! Whoever does the will of God is my brother and sister and mother" (3:33–34).

Jesus does not specify what doing the will of God consists of, but presumably one might assume that at the least it entails being with Jesus and, as the parables that follow indicate, listening to and taking to heart his teaching. Later in the Gospel, Peter, James, and John will hear a voice from heaven instruct them, regarding Jesus, "This is my Son, the Beloved: *listen to him*" (9:7). Here Jesus reconstitutes his "family" as those who are around him, a group that presumably includes his disciples, but is not restricted to them.

The parabolic teaching that follows immediately upon this incident is important for comprehending the Gospel's understanding of the requirements for true discipleship, and we shall have to return to it below. For the moment, we note that the initial telling of the parable of the sower (4:3–9) and its subsequent explanation (4:14–20) are separated by a note that Jesus withdraws from the crowd he has been teaching. The narrator states that "*those who were around him along with the twelve*" ask him about the parables (note the plural). Hence what Jesus says next is directed at the twelve named and identified disciples, but not at them alone. There is also a wider circle, "those who were around him," who are included. What Jesus tells them is that they have been given "the secret of the kingdom of God" (4:11).

"But," Jesus goes on, "for those outside, everything comes in parables, in order that

> "they may indeed look, but not perceive,
> and may indeed listen, but not understand;
> so that they may not turn again and be forgiven."
> (4:12)

Who are "those outside"? Well, we have already been informed that Jesus' own natural family was standing *outside* when they came to get him. And they have demonstrated their "outsider" status in that they do not accept that his activity arises from anything other than that he is "out of his mind" (3:21). We must presume, also, that most of the large crowd who heard Jesus' parable of the sower are also "outsiders," as Jesus has retreated to a more private teaching session with the twelve and "those around him."

While there is an indeterminate penumbra of people (members of "the crowd") who often receive Jesus' teaching about discipleship, "the twelve" and the disciples represent the paradigmatic group of Jesus' followers whose performance and progress in discipleship the reader may evaluate as the story proceeds. Initially, as we have seen, the reader is likely to form a positive impression of their discipleship. But there are ominous signs that soon emerge. In fact, in the very locale of 4:10–12, where Jesus pronounces the twelve to be "insiders" who have the secret of the kingdom, the first sign that all is not well in this regard emerges. For Jesus then says, "Do you not understand this parable? Then how will you understand all the parables?" It seems that these "insiders" themselves struggle to understand the drift of Jesus' important parable.

From this point on, the disciples begin to appear in a more and more ambiguous light. They struggle to understand both who Jesus is and the nature of discipleship.

Following Jesus on the Way

On the evening of the day on which Jesus teaches these parables, he and his disciples are caught up in a storm on Lake Galilee. When the disciples, terrified that they are about to drown, wake a sleeping Jesus, he calms the storm, then asks them why they are afraid and without faith. If the disciples were afraid before, they are even more afraid now (the Greek might be translated, "they feared with a great fear"), and say to one another, "Who then is this, that even the wind and the sea obey him?"

It is one of the implied author's narrative "tricks" that no answer is provided to this question. It hangs in the air for the reader to resolve. If we may imagine the disciples recalling Psalm 107:23–29[4], then we may also imagine that their great awe was occasioned by the unspoken question, "If this person can calm the storm, can he be God?" This inter-textual association is certainly available to the reader, and perhaps the implied author intended the reader to recall it.

Whether or not this is so, the story proceeds, and when the disciples are dispatched on their mission, and before their return is narrated, the implied author employs the sandwich technique to relate the death of John the Baptist. In fact, this story is an example of *analepsis*, a technique whereby information is provided later for an event mentioned earlier. In Mark 1:14, the narrator mentions that John had been arrested. Now the story which explains the

---

4. "Some went down to the sea in ships, doing business of the mighty waters; they saw the deeds of the Lord, his wondrous works in the deep. For he commanded and raised the stormy wind, which lifted up the waves of the sea. They mounted to the heaven, they went down to the depths; their courage melted away in their calamity; they reeled and staggered like drunkards, and were at their wits' end. Then they cried to the Lord in their trouble, and he brought them out of their distress; he made the storm be still, and the waves of the sea were hushed" (NRSV).

reason for his arrest and his subsequent fate is narrated. The upshot of the story is that John is beheaded. This story is seen by many scholars as told to parallel and anticipate the eventual fate of Jesus. If this is the case then the note at the end of the story that John's disciples came and took John's body and laid it in a tomb is significant. No such action is undertaken by Jesus' disciples after his death.

As the story continues, the reader learns of the way in which the disciples are challenged by Jesus to provide food for five thousand people, after they have urged Jesus to send them away so that they might find provisions in the surrounding villages. The disciples are stumped, and reckon they will need two hundred *denarii* (about two hundred days' worth of a basic wage) to feed the crowd. However, Jesus feeds the crowd with five loaves and two fish that they have on hand, and the disciples find that there are twelve baskets of leftovers remaining.

Immediately upon the conclusion of this feeding miracle, Jesus makes the disciples get into a boat to cross the lake while he remains alone to pray. The disciples find themselves making little headway against an adverse wind, and in the early morning see Jesus walking on the water. They are terrified thinking that they are seeing a ghost, until Jesus reassures them as he identifies himself, climbs into the boat, and the wind ceases. Despite the earlier experience of Jesus stilling the storm, the disciples are astounded. The narrator adds a cryptic comment: "for they did not understand about the loaves, but their hearts were hardened" (6:52).

What the disciples are supposed to understand on account of the provision of much bread is not made clear, though the disciples are expected to draw some conclusions from the feeding miracle about Jesus' identity. The fact that "their hearts were hardened" ought to unsettle the

Following Jesus on the Way

reader, for it suggests that they may prove to be a poor sort of "soil" (see below). Shortly thereafter, the narrator again tells a story about a feeding miracle, which he introduces with the words: "In those days when there was again a great crowd without anything to eat . . ." (8:1). Jesus has compassion on the crowd, and is concerned that if he sends them away hungry they will faint on the way. His words imply that he would like to do something about supplying them with food, for the disciples reply, "How can one feed these people with bread here in the desert?"

The disciples, the reader may surmise, give every indication of having forgotten about the previous occasion upon which Jesus fed a great crowd with only meager rations on hand. Once again he asks them how many loaves they have, and they reply that they have seven. On this occasion, four thousand people are fed and seven baskets of leftovers are collected. Then Jesus and his disciples climb into a boat and cross the lake. After a brief interchange with some Pharisees who are after a sign from heaven (a request the reader, at least, will find ironic, given the number of "signs" that have been narrated), Jesus and the disciples re-embark and head back across the lake.

Now the disciples' lack of understanding and incomprehension is brought to a head in a highly charged interchange (8:14–21). The reader is told that they have forgotten to bring any bread, apart, that is, from one loaf. Jesus proceeds to warn them against the "yeast" of the Pharisees and of Herod. What Jesus means by this is not made clear: but, at any rate, the disciples think that Jesus must be having a sly dig at them for not remembering to bring bread. When Jesus becomes aware of this, he asks: "Why are you talking about having no bread? Do you still not perceive or understand? Are your hearts hardened? Do you have eyes, and fail to see? Do you have ears and fail to hear?" (8:17–18).

These questions unsettle the reader, and raise sharp questions about the disciples' status as "insiders." This is because the lines about eyes and ears evoke the quotation from Isaiah 6:9–10 which Jesus uses in Mark 4:12 to explain why "those outside" receive everything in parables. Here are "insiders," privy to the "secret of the kingdom," suffering from the condition that afflicts "outsiders." Once again the question is raised whether they have hard hearts. Jesus then reminds them of the outcome of the two feeding stories. When the five thousand were fed with five loaves, how many baskets of leftovers were collected up? Like a class of young elementary schoolchildren the disciples chorus, "Twelve." When the four thousand were fed with seven loaves, how many baskets then? "Seven" reply the disciples. This is high comedy in a deadly serious situation.

"Do you not yet understand?" Jesus asks. Once again, here is a question without an answer in the story. The reader must supply the answer: and it would appear that the answer must be, no, the disciples do not yet understand. What the disciples are to understand is likewise obscure. Perhaps it is simply that having fed five thousand with five loaves, and four thousand with seven loaves, the disciples should not be concerned that one loaf will be insufficient. At this point in the story, at virtually the midpoint of the Gospel, the reader is left with the uneasy sense that insiders really are outsiders.

A PARABLE FOR LEARNERS: "IF YOU HAVE EARS, LISTEN UP!"

Scholars note that it is in Mark's Gospel that Jesus is most often referred to as a teacher. In the Gospel, there are two places where he provides sustained teaching. The first of these is in Mark chapter 4, where Jesus teaches in parables. Two parables are about the nature of the kingdom of God. But the first parable is a parable about being a learner, and about the conditions required for ensuring that one is ready to receive Jesus' teaching. This parable is conventionally called "the parable of the sower": and that it is about listening is underscored by the fact that Jesus prefaces his telling of it with the word, "Listen!" and concludes with the advice, "Let anyone with ears to hear listen!" (4:9).

Furthermore, it is a parable with an explanation (4:14–20). And this explanation turns the parable into an allegory about different types of receptivity to Jesus' teaching. The setting in which Jesus delivers this parable is significant. He begins to teach beside the lake but because the crowd is very large Jesus gets into a boat and teaches from there, one imagines some distance off shore. Meanwhile the crowd is standing "beside the lake on the land." The Greek word used here for land (*gē*), is the same one used for "earth" or "soil" in the parable, as when Jesus speaks of "rocky ground" that does not have "much soil," where the seed sprouts quickly because there is "no depth of soil" (v. 5), and of the "good soil" (v. 8). As it is "the word" that the sower sows according to the allegory, we may think of Jesus in the boat throwing his words (like the sower) out onto the land where the people stand, no doubt in various states of receptivity.

The allegory, then, reveals that there are various types of receptivity (different soils) to the word, or the teaching that Jesus gives. One type of hearer is like a hard-beaten path, where the seed (teaching) cannot penetrate and is quickly removed by Satan. Are these to be described as hearers whose hearts are hard? This is worrying, for the disciples prove to be those whose hearts are hard (6:52; 8:17c).

Other hearers receive the teaching eagerly, but they prove to be "rocky ground" with no depth of soil. The teaching cannot take root, and so when the teaching proves to bring trouble or persecution, they abandon their adherence to it. A third type of hearer hears the teaching alright, and they may even take it to heart, but there are other things that prevent it from being effective in their lives. They are distracted by cares and worries, or by "the lure of wealth," or the desire for things other than provided for by the teaching.

Finally there are those who "hear the word and accept it." They are like "good soil" for they allow the teaching to take root and bear fruit. These ones are those whose listening yields results that are amazing. Any Palestinian farmer in the first century, who would consider a tenfold yield on his crop a good harvest, would be absolutely delighted if not incredulous to have crops that yielded thirtyfold, let alone sixty- and a hundredfold. A New Zealand sheep farmer might speak of lambing percentages of 130, 160, and 200 percent (though 230, 260, and 300 percent might better capture the character of the figures in the parable!).

That the parable is placed here to alert the reader to the importance of the character of their listening for their understanding of Jesus teaching and for their discipleship is underscored by the words Jesus speaks to "those around him along with the twelve." The counterpoint to being given "the secret of the kingdom of God" is to receive "everything" in parables. It would seem that Jesus speaks in parables "in order that [quoting Isaiah] 'they may indeed look, but not perceive, and may indeed listen, but not understand; so that they may not turn again and be forgiven'" (4:12). It is almost as if Jesus suggests that he speaks in parables in order to confuse, and to prevent "those outside" from grasping and understanding his teaching, lest they should come to a position of turning to God and being forgiven.

Following Jesus on the Way

Scholars debate the force of the words "in order that" (Greek: *hina*) and the "so that" (Greek: *mēpote*) and whether they have the effect of indicating that the intention is to prevent understanding and ensuring a lack of a positive response to God. I think that the quotation can be understood ironically. The "so that" might be better translated "lest" or "otherwise." In other words, if people were not so willfully imperceptive and lacking in understanding, they would, in fact, turn to God who would forgive them. This is the sense in which the text in Isaiah can be understood, I believe, and in the Septuagint (the Greek Old Testament) Isaiah 6:10 can be translated something like this: "Make the heart of this people impervious [or, dull] and their ears hard of hearing, and their eyes closed, otherwise [or, lest] their eyes might see and their ears might hear and [their] heart might comprehend thoroughly and they might turn and I will heal them."[5]

Whatever the case, Jesus wants his hearers to understand that how they listen and the effort they make to understand is vitally important. Nothing should be taken for granted. In a couple of cryptic sayings he underscores the importance of listening well. Lamps are for a lampstand so that they can shed their light abroad; they are not to be hidden under "the bushel basket." Just so, ears are for listening. But, more to the point, the purpose of the teaching is not ultimately to conceal, but to be understood by those who are perceptive.[6] What is hidden or currently a secret because not understood is to be disclosed and brought to

---

5. Isa 6:10 in the NRSV reads: "Make the mind of this people dull, and stop their ears, and shut their eyes, so that they may not look with their eyes, and listen with their ears, and comprehend with their minds, and turn *and be healed*" (italics mine).

6. Collins, *Mark*, 253, makes a nice point here: "There will always be outsiders who will reject the proclamation, but the circle of insiders is an open, not a closed one."

light (4:21–22). Jesus emphasizes the point by repeating the injunction with which he concluded the parable of the sower. "Let anyone with ears to hear listen!" (4:23).

He continues with his second cryptic saying: "Pay attention to what you hear; the measure you give will be the measure you get, and still more will be given to you. For to those who have, more will be given; and from those who have nothing, even what they have will be taken away" (4:24–25). Herein, perhaps, is the answer to the riddle of 4:12. If you are dull and uncomprehending, if you have no desire to understand or make no effort to listen and take to heart Jesus' teaching, then even what little chance of understanding you may have will disappear. Certainly, the seed that falls on the hard, beaten path does not remain there for long. It is soon snatched away by the birds: just as "the word," or teaching, that is not received will be immediately taken away by Satan, the adversary of spiritual comprehension.

A SEMINAR ON DISCIPLESHIP

The reader who has followed the story of Jesus and the disciples to the midpoint of the story has learned much about both Jesus and the disciples. The reader has observed Jesus performing miracles and exorcisms, and has seen how these have raised questions about who Jesus is in the minds of other characters, the disciples included. The reader has also seen the disciples in a light that initially paints a positive picture of their discipleship, but then becomes increasingly ambiguous and murky. They seem be more like outsiders than insiders, as their comprehension of who Jesus is and what he wishes to convey to them appears to be less and less certain. The reader has also heard Jesus deliver some teaching on the importance of being receptive hearers and

Following Jesus on the Way

retentive learners of his teaching. These qualities are vital for disciples.

From Mark 8:27 to 10:45 Jesus embarks on what I like to call "a seminar on messiahship and discipleship." In this part of the Gospel, Jesus delivers some teaching on what it means to be the Christ, and what it means to be followers of the Christ. On three separate occasions he is represented as teaching the disciples about what is to happen to him in the future. Scholars have noticed that each of these occasions follows a repeating pattern. First, Jesus issues what is commonly described as a "passion prediction," that is, he tells the disciples that the time is coming when he (the Son of Man) will be put to death by the Jewish leaders, but will rise again after three days. This is followed by some sort of "misunderstanding" on the part of the disciples, or behavior on their part that shows that their interests and concerns do not match Jesus' agenda. In response, Jesus embarks on a clarification of what it means to be a disciple. This repeating pattern of passion prediction, misunderstanding, and clarification is found in Mark 8:31–38; 9:30–37; and 10:35–45. We will consider each in turn.

The threefold seminar is introduced by Jesus asking a couple of significant questions of the disciples. In Mark 8:27 the narrator tells the reader that "Jesus went on with his disciples to the villages of Caesarea Philippi." In view of the questions Jesus is about to ask, the location, in the vicinity of Caesarea Philippi, where he poses these questions is significant. Near Caesarea Philippi there was a cave dedicated to the god, Pan, who had played an important role in the ruler cults of the Syrian-Greek dynasty of the Ptolemies, and perhaps the Seleucids, as well. In 20 BCE the region was given to Herod the Great by Caesar Augustus. Herod, in gratitude, built a temple in white marble and dedicated it to Augustus. After Herod's death, his son Philip built a city near the cave and called it Caesarea (Philippi was added to the name to distinguish it from other cities called Caesarea).[7]

In this region, where politics and religion combined in cultic worship, Jesus asks his disciples what people are saying about him. They give a variety of opinions: some say he is John the Baptist, others that he is Elijah, still others that he is "one of the prophets." In fact, the narrator had earlier reported this range of opinions in introducing the story of the death of John the Baptist (see 6:14–16). "Well, then," Jesus goes on, "who do *you* say that I am?" (8:29). Peter replies, "You are the Messiah (or, Christ)." It would seem that Peter at least (though he is probably acting here as a spokesperson for all the disciples), now clearly understands, and has correctly identified, who Jesus is. The reader will recall that the narrator began this story by identifying Jesus as the Christ.

Jesus immediately begins his first "seminar session." The narrator informs us that "he began to teach them that the Son of Man must undergo great suffering, and be rejected by the elders, the chief priests, and the scribes, and be killed, and after three days rise again" (8:31). And for good measure, the narrator adds, "He said all this quite openly" (8:32b). But Peter is not happy with this teaching. He takes Jesus aside and begins to remonstrate with him. Jesus in turn rebukes Peter (and the narrator indicates that this is a public rebuke, directed at Peter, but intended for all the disciples). "Get behind me, Satan! For you are setting your mind not on divine things but on human things."[8]

These are strong words. What has gone wrong: how is it that Peter, who seems to have correctly identified who Jesus is (after all, Jesus does not contradict Peter, but enjoins

7. See Collins, *Mark*, 399–400; and also Culpepper, *Mark*, 266.
8. "You are not on the side of God, but of men" (RSV).

Following Jesus on the Way

all the disciples to silence on the matter), can so quickly be offside with Jesus? What is it that he does not *now* understand? The point is that while Peter understands that Jesus is the Messiah, he does not understand, or is not prepared to accept, what it means for Jesus to be the Messiah. Jesus is speaking of suffering and death. Jesus indicates that as the Messiah, he will be rejected by the Jewish leadership. This does not figure in Peter's understanding of what it means to be the Messiah. There is a standoff: and Jesus indicates that Peter's perspective is not that of God, but is purely human. If Peter cannot accept that as the Messiah Jesus must suffer, and die, then he is on the side of Satan, not of God. He is an adversary to Jesus, not a disciple.

So Jesus begins to teach about discipleship. Notice that this teaching is not confined to his disciples. As we have already seen, there is often a penumbra of people around the inner circle of the disciples (see, e.g., 3:34; 4:10) who are included in Jesus' teaching: and who also receive the challenge to be disciples. This teaching is foundational to the nature of discipleship, according to Mark's Gospel. Anyone who wishes to become a follower of Jesus must be prepared to deny himself, or herself, and take up the cross. Jesus' way is the way to, or of, the cross: and those who follow him must go that way as well. Seek to save one's life, and one will lose it. Lose one's life for the sake of Jesus and the gospel, and it will be saved. Otherwise one might find that one may gain "the whole world" but find one's life forfeit: and what can one then give to get it back? This is tough, uncompromising teaching. It is difficult to accept today: it was just as difficult then.

It should be noted that this teaching about following "the way of Jesus" is delivered while Jesus and his disciples are "on the way." They are "on the way" when Jesus asks his two significant questions. They are "on the way," passing through Galilee, when Jesus takes up the "seminar on messiahship and discipleship" a second time (see Mark 9:30–32). The teaching is terse: "The Son of Man is to be betrayed into human hands, and they will kill him, and three days after being killed, he will rise again." The disciples do not understand him, and they are afraid to ask him. Are they giving up on this difficult topic? Are they preoccupied with other matters?

Perhaps it is the latter: for when they arrive at their destination, Capernaum, Jesus asks them what they were arguing about "on the way." The rift between Jesus and the disciples is beginning to show: he has not been privy to their conversation. They, sensing that their agenda will not be shared by Jesus, are reluctant to divulge what they have been bickering about: which one of them is the greatest.

Their "misunderstanding" of the nature of discipleship prompts Jesus into further teaching for clarification. "Whoever wants to be first must be last of all and servant of all." This time he provides a visual aid. He takes a little child in his arms: perhaps it is a baby, perhaps he gathers up a toddler onto his lap? Whatever the case, in first-century Jewish society, one could not find a human being more lacking in status and importance than a little child. The child in Jesus' arms was a symbol of insignificance. Jesus goes on, "Whoever welcomes one such child in my name welcomes me, and whoever welcomes me welcomes not me but the one who sent me" (Mark 9:33).

These words are apparently lost on the disciples. They remain fixated upon "rights" and "who's in and who's out." Someone, they discover, has been casting out demons in Jesus' name. As John reports it, "We tried to stop him, because he was not following us" (9:38). Not following them? Are they not disciples of Jesus: and is not Jesus a teacher whose invitation to discipleship is open to all who will take

Following Jesus on the Way

on his program? A further irony is that the disciples, once dispatched by Jesus to cast out demons (6:6b), something they appeared to have been able to do quite successfully (6:13), have, on their last attempt at exorcism, been quite unable to achieve a good result (see 9:18). In respect of this unknown exorcist, Jesus soon puts his disciples right. Furthermore, anyone who performs a simple act of service for them because they "bear the name of Christ will by no means lose the reward" (9:41). But a discipleship of being hospitable is beyond the disciples, and despite Jesus' words about welcoming a child, they are soon busy turning little children away. Jesus' indignant response provides a further lesson in what it means to be a disciple. "Let the little children come to me; do not stop them; for it is to *such as these* that the kingdom of God belongs. Truly I tell you, whoever does not receive the kingdom of God as a little child will never enter it" (10:15).

This episode in which Jesus blesses little children is followed by a story of a rich man who runs up to Jesus as he is setting out on a journey. The man has a significant question to ask about how to inherit eternal life. The interchange soon hones in upon the central issue. Will this man follow Jesus on the way? He is a man of integrity, who has lived an upright life, maintaining right relations with his fellow humans. Jesus regards him with love, and issues the challenge: "You lack one thing: go, sell what you own, and give the money to the poor, and you will have treasure in heaven; then come, follow me" (10:21). The man is shocked by this challenge. Finding himself unable to take it up, he departs sorrowfully. The reason for his response, the narrator informs us, is that he has many possessions. Jesus' word to him has fallen among "thorns," choked by "the lure of wealth and the desire for other things" (see 4:18–19).

His departure causes Jesus to comment on the difficulty that those who have wealth will have in entering the kingdom of God. The narrator says that before Jesus makes this comment he looks around and then speaks to the disciples. This action on Jesus' part is a good indication that what he has to say bears some importance for the issue of discipleship (see also 3:34; 8:33). It is the disciples' turn to be shocked: especially when Jesus reiterates the point, using a striking comparison, "It is easier for a camel to go through the eye of a needle than for someone who is rich to enter the kingdom of God" (10:25). In consternation, they turn to one another and ask, "Then who can be saved?" It is impossible, Jesus concedes, for humans: but not for God.

Peter now wishes to point out the extent of their own sacrifice in following Jesus. "Look," says he, "we have left everything and followed you" (10:28). "Indeed," Jesus replies, "but in truth, anyone who leaves house, or family, or property for my sake and the good news, will find those things returned to them (as it were) a hundred times over in this life; and in the next life, will receive eternal life." But there is a sting in the tail: in this life, those things will all be returned, "with persecutions." John Donahue suggests that this passage relates in part to the "new family" into which disciples enter (see again Mark 3:31–34). He writes: "Leaving parents, abandoning occupations and the pursuit of wealth, observance of Jesus' teaching on divorce, consideration for children—all these would bring Christians into conflict with the prevailing ethos and values and evoke that kind of suspicion and hatred which meant that the possession of new mothers, brothers and sisters would exist only 'with persecutions.'"[9] In conclusion, Jesus returns to a theme which he conveyed in his clarification following the second passion prediction, with its attendant misunderstanding on

9. Donahue, *Theology and Setting of Discipleship*, 46.

the part of the disciples. "Many who are first will be last, and the last will be first" (10:31).

So Jesus embarks upon his third and final passion prediction, and the third of his "seminar sessions." Now the direction of the journey is made clear: they are on the road, going up to Jerusalem (10:32). The narrator indicates the consternation and the fear that grips those who are following Jesus. Evidently this is a larger group than just the twelve disciples: Jesus takes these twelve aside and outlines what will happen in Jerusalem. This passion prediction is the most detailed of the three, and functions as a summary of what will happen to Jesus later in the story. He will be betrayed to the Jewish leadership, who will condemn him to death; they in turn will hand him over to the Roman authorities, who will mock him, spit on him, flog him, and, finally, kill him. After three days he will rise again.

All of this is like water off a duck's back, at least as far as James and John, the sons of Zebedee, are concerned. They make a power play. They presume to ask Jesus to grant them "whatever we ask of you," which amounts to a request for the two positions of most importance when Jesus establishes the kingdom (his kingdom, they assume) and sits "in [his] glory" (10:36). They may have abandoned "everything" to follow Jesus: but they have not abandoned their ambitions. They would like to have the most important portfolios in the Cabinet, as it were.

They do not know what they are asking, Jesus replies. "Are you able to drink the cup that I drink, or be baptized with the baptism that I am baptized with?" he asks (10:34). Jesus is referring to his impending death. "We are able," James and John reply airily. Perhaps this is bravado, perhaps it arises from their real ignorance of what lies ahead. Whatever is the case, Jesus assures them that they will indeed experience what he is about to experience. But it is not within his purview to grant what they wish.

The other ten disciples learn of the brothers' request. They are furious. Not, one suspects, because James and John were so foolish as to make such a request after all Jesus' teaching about the last being first, and the kingdom being for those who become like children. No, they are cross that James and John tried to steal a march on the rest of them. None of them have taken any of Jesus' teachings to heart.

Now Jesus once more clarifies matters: and this time he is quite direct. The way of Gentile rulers is to "lord it over" their subjects and their great ones are tyrants. "But it is not so among you," Jesus states firmly. Those who wish to be great must become a servant to the others. Whoever wishes to be first must be slave of all. Now Jesus delivers a statement which might be described as "the gospel in a nutshell." It certainly drives home the point he is making: "For [even] the Son of Man came not to be served but to serve, and to give his life as ransom for many" (10:45). On that note the seminar series comes to an end.

A BRACKET OF HEALINGS: TWO BLIND MEN

At this point it is important to notice a particular feature of the way in which the implied author has structured his story. The section of the Gospel that we have been considering, in which appear the three "seminar sessions on messiahship and discipleship," has been bracketed by the stories of the healing of blind men. Immediately before Jesus asks the two significant questions which introduce the seminar sessions, the narrator recounts the healing of a blind man (8:22–26). Again, straight after Jesus has finished the clarification following the misunderstanding of the disciples in

Following Jesus on the Way

the wake of his third passion prediction, the narrator relates the healing of a blind man called Bartimaeus (10:46–52). Hence, these stories are like "bookends" around this part of the story, a central section in the plot, and one in which the movement of Jesus is, in retrospect, understood to entail a journey from Galilee to Jerusalem.

The first healing story contains a very interesting feature. It is the only story of a healing in this Gospel (or indeed any of the Gospels) where Jesus' first attempt at healing is not fully successful. A blind man is brought to him, and, after leading him out of the village, Jesus puts saliva on his eyes, lays his hands on him and asks, "Can you see anything?" (8:23). "I can see people," the man replies, "but they look like trees, walking." He can see, but not clearly. His vision remains blurred. The narrator recounts how Jesus lays his hands on the man's eyes again. This time, the narrator informs the reader, the man "looked intently and his sight was restored, and he saw everything clearly" (8:25).

Why? What is the purpose of this two-stage healing? It is widely recognized that this story may function as a symbol of the stage at which the disciples have arrived in their understanding at this point in the Gospel. They have grasped something of who Jesus is, but they do not clearly understand who he is or what his program entails. This is borne out in the story that follows of the interchange between Jesus and Peter. Peter is able to correctly identify Jesus as the Christ. But Peter is not able to understand, or "see," what it means for Jesus to be the Christ. He cannot follow Jesus on the way to the cross: at least, not with clear-sighted comprehension. He can only stumble along, as do others, in fear and confusion, often amazed, astounded, and shocked.

At the conclusion of the "seminar on the road," Jesus and the disciples come to Jericho, on the way to Jerusalem.

As they leave the city, there is a commotion. A blind man, Bartimaeus son of Timaeus, sitting by the road begging, learns that Jesus is passing by. He begins to shout loudly, "Jesus, Son of David, have mercy on me!" (10:47). Many try to silence him, but he will not be silenced. He shouts even louder, so that Jesus stops and says, "Call him here." When Bartimaeus arrives before him, Jesus asks him, "What do you want me to do for you?" "My teacher," Bartimaeus replies, "let me see again." "Go," Jesus says to him, "your faith has made you well." Immediately, Bartimaeus regains his sight. But he does not go, as Jesus orders him to: rather, he follows Jesus on the way.

Scholars recognize that a number of details in this story indicate that Bartimaeus may be taken as an exemplar of discipleship.[10] In the first place, when Jesus stops because of Bartimaeus's loud shouting, he says, "Call him here." Thus Bartimaeus is one called by Jesus, just as James and John were called (1:20); this is reinforced by the encouragement of the bystanders who tell the blind man to take heart because Jesus is calling him. Second, when called, Bartimaeus throws off his cloak, leaps up, and goes to Jesus. A beggar's most prized possession would be his cloak. It also represents his old life and occupation. Like the first disciples, Bartimaeus leaves his occupation behind and goes to Jesus. Third, in response to Jesus' question, Bartimaeus prefaces his reply by addressing Jesus as "My Teacher." "Teacher" (in the Greek it is "Rabbi") is the title a disciple would call his master. So, finally, Bartimaeus, his sight restored, follows Jesus on the way. And, as noted above, at this point in the story, the way of Jesus is most definitely the way to Jerusalem, and hence the way to his cross.

---

10. The fact that Bartimaeus is named is an interesting feature. Does this mean that this story recalls an actual person who was known to the community to which the Gospel was directed?

Following Jesus on the Way

There is a further feature of this story that links it with the passage before it. James and John, and Bartimaeus, each want Jesus to do something for them. In each case, Jesus' first question to them is the same: "What do you want me to do for you?" (10:36, 51). But James and John's request is not one a disciple should ask. Jesus can accede to Bartimaeus's request, but not to theirs. The fact that Bartimaeus's story provides a bookend with the story of the other unnamed blind man told at the start of this part of the Gospel, raises a question over how the disciples have fared in their learning. Have they moved from half-understanding, and blurred vision, to a full and proper comprehension that affords clear sight; or do they remain half-blind and still lacking in understanding?

"ALL OF THEM DESERTED HIM AND FLED" (MARK 14:50)

In fact, the reader discovers, reading on, that the disciples remain fallible followers. Indeed, in many respects, their relationship with Jesus goes from bad to worse. The reader will discover by the end of the story that Judas has betrayed Jesus, and Peter has denied him. The four disciples who were called first are given some private teaching by Jesus (in Mark 13), in the course of which they are warned to keep awake (13:35, 37). Later, in the Garden of Gethsemane, the first three named of these four, namely, Peter, James, and John, are taken apart by Jesus and asked to keep awake while he prays in anguish nearby. They fail to do so. The first time that Jesus returns and finds them sleeping, he says to Peter, "Keep awake and pray that you may not come into the time of trial" (14:38; in the Greek, though Jesus addresses Peter, the verb forms are all those for the second person plural, so we might understand Jesus to say, "You all keep awake . . ."). Three times Jesus returns to find them sleeping. When he returns the third time, the time of trial is indeed upon them.

When the arresting party arrives, it is led by Judas who chooses to provide a particularly cynical signal to indicate their man to the armed crowd. He calls Jesus "Rabbi," and gives him the kiss of friendship. The narrator concludes the account of the arrest with this terse observation: "All of them [that is, the disciples] deserted him and fled." There follows a small and puzzling cameo scene. "A certain young man" has been following Jesus.[11] He is clothed only in a linen cloth. When the arresting party seize him, he manages to escape by slipping free of his linen covering, and fleeing away naked. He is paradigmatic of the disciples at this point. To flee naked, is to flee ashamed and utterly discredited. The disciples are such "naked" followers of Jesus.

From this point in the story, the male disciples do not again appear. Apart from Peter, that is, who follows Jesus (and the arresting party) "at a distance" into the courtyard of the high priest, where he sits around a fire with the guards warming himself (14:54). The implied author employs the sandwich technique here, for having placed Peter outside, in the courtyard, he moves the scene inside where Jesus is being interrogated. Now Jesus, when asked point blank by the high priest whether he is "the Messiah, the Son of the Blessed One," states clearly, and unequivocally, "I am" (14:61–62).

---

11. The identity of this young man has been a source of fascination, and speculation among commentators (and readers generally). A common understanding is that this young man is a literary representation of the actual author (often taken to be John Mark, see Acts 12:12) who gives himself a "bit part" in his story, rather like Peter Jackson, the producer of the films *The Lord of the Rings*, or as Alfred Hitchcock was apparently in the habit of doing in his films. I prefer to see him as a symbolic figure.

Following Jesus on the Way

Having struggled to find witnesses whose testimony against Jesus is consistent, the high priest is able to declare that they can dispense with witnesses, as in their eyes Jesus now stands self-condemned of blasphemy. He is condemned to death. But before proceeding to the next stage, which will be to hand him over to Pilate, the Roman Governor, so that he can be charged with a capital offence, some of them insult and hit Jesus. They blindfold Jesus and, striking him, call upon him to "prophesy!" (14:65).

In a scene fraught with irony, Jesus' prophecy (14:30) that Peter would deny him three times before the cock crows twice begins to play out in the courtyard below, as Peter is accosted by one of the servant girls of the high priest. When she states that Peter was with Jesus, Peter denies it. "I do not know or understand what you are talking about," he remonstrates. That Peter lacks knowledge and understanding is a fair summary of where his discipleship now stands. Accosted twice more over his relationship with Jesus, Peter each time denies it, the third time cursing and swearing. The cock crows a second time, and Peter remembers Jesus' words. The narrator's comment is poignant, but final: "And he broke down and wept." That is where the story leaves Peter, distraught at the realization that what Jesus said is true. His discipleship has failed.

The discipleship of all the named disciples ("the Twelve") has proven to end in failure. This situation is made even more stark by the fact that the implied author provides exemplars of good discipleship, and of what it means to be a disciple in some of the minor characters that appear. We have already considered Bartimaeus. In the latter chapters of the Gospel, we may identify at least four more.

One is a poor widow whom Jesus observes putting two small coins into the temple treasury (see 12:41–44). Meanwhile, the narrator informs the reader, "Many rich people put in large sums." Seeing this, Jesus calls his disciples (note this, it signals that an important point will be made). He says to them, "Truly I tell you [Greek: *amēn*, a further indication that an important point will be made], this poor widow has put in more than all those who are contributing to the treasury. For all of them have contributed out of their abundance; but she out of her poverty has put in everything she had, all she had to live on" (12:43–44). "Everything she had" and "all she had to live on": the rich man, seeking "eternal life" and challenged to follow Jesus earlier was unable to relinquish his "everything" (10:21–22). What does it profit anyone to gain the whole world and forfeit his, or her, life (8:36)? "Look, we have left everything and followed you," claims Peter (10:28). But trials and "persecution" have now come, and Peter has "fallen away" (see 4:17).

Another paradigm of discipleship comes as the dark clouds of the story of Jesus' death begin to form. Jesus is having a meal at the home of "Simon the leper" when an unnamed woman comes to the table with an alabaster jar of very expensive ointment of nard which she proceeds to pour on Jesus' head (14:3–9). This creates indignation among some who are there, who consider that the money that this ointment could have fetched would have been better spent on aiding the poor. But Jesus defends her. She has performed a "good service" for him. Good service is what disciples are called upon to give (another who serves is Peter's mother-in-law who, once healed by Jesus of her fever, "began to serve them"; see 1:29–31). Moreover, this woman not only acts as a prophet who "anoints" the Messiah, but also anticipates Jesus' death and burial. "Truly [*amēn*] I tell you," Jesus concludes, "wherever the good news is proclaimed in the whole world, what she has done will be told in remembrance of her."

Following Jesus on the Way

Two named characters, in even briefer cameo scenes, fulfill the role of disciples. Simon of Cyrene is press-ganged into carrying Jesus' cross (15:21). He represents the call to carry the cross of Jesus. And after Jesus' death, Joseph of Arimathea, one who is described as "waiting expectantly for the kingdom of God," boldly asks Pilate for the body of Jesus. He then buries the body: a task that the disciples should attend to, but they are nowhere to be found.

But perhaps all is not lost. Jesus' male disciples have fled; they are nowhere to be seen as Jesus dies on the cross. But the reader discovers that there is a group of women who are looking on "from a distance" (15:40–41). Three of these are identified by name; they are Mary Magdalene, Mary the mother of James the younger and of Joses, and Salome.[12] Now the reader discovers that they, too, are disciples, for the language of discipleship is used of them. They "used to follow him." Furthermore, they were with Jesus in Galilee, the place where he fulfilled his ministry, and where his male disciples were schooled in the art of discipleship. These women "provided for" Jesus: the inference is that they served Jesus. Now they observe Jesus' crucifixion, and his burial. R. Alan Culpepper notes that "in the Gospel narrative, they stand in where the disciples should have been and perform the tasks the disciples should have done. They are therefore faithful (to a point—see 16:8) in spite of the fact that they were marginalized by society."[13] As were children, we might add.

---

12. The second Mary is sometimes identified as being the mother of Jesus, on account of the fact that she is said to be the "mother of James and Joses" (who are taken to be Jesus' brothers mentioned by these names in 6:3). Collins, *Mark*, 774, does not share this view; and it does seem that such an identification undercuts the earlier dismissal of Jesus' family (3:31–35).

13. Culpepper, *Mark*, 576.

These women, on the day following the Sabbath, proceed to the tomb in order to fulfill a last act of service: they intend to anoint Jesus' body. But the body of Jesus is not there. Instead they find an open tomb, and inside a young man, dressed in a white robe, who makes an astounding announcement and commissions them with a message for the (male) disciples.[14] "Do not be alarmed; you are looking for Jesus of Nazareth, who was crucified. He has been raised; he is not here. Look, there is the place they laid him. But go, tell his disciples and Peter that he is going ahead of you to Galilee; there you will see him, just as he told you."

The inclusion of Peter separately in the message is a nice touch. Peter, perhaps hiding away from the other disciples in shame, requires special reassurance that he is still included. There is hope: the resurrection of Jesus is clearly signaled ("He has been raised: he is not here"). There is a promise that they will meet Jesus again, in Galilee (note that the women are included both in the promise that they will see Jesus in Galilee and that it will be as Jesus told them). It remains for the women to deliver the message. But here the story fails: indeed, here these women disciples also fail. The story ends on an open and puzzling note: "So they went out and fled from the tomb, for terror and amazement had seized them; and they said nothing to anyone, for they were afraid" (16:8).

THE PURPOSE OF THE PUZZLING ENDING: BACK TO GALILEE . . .

What is the reader to make of this ending to the implied author's portrayal of the disciples as fallible and failing?

14. Is this young man, robed in white, a symbolic counter to the young man who flees away naked (Mark 14:52)? Might he be a sign of hope: a reversal of that shameful condition?

Following Jesus on the Way

If the women say nothing to anyone, do the disciples ever receive the message? The male disciples have failed in their discipleship: now the women disciples appear also to have failed. What is the author's purpose here? How is the reader to understand the story of the disciples in the light of this ending? Scholars have given a variety of answers to the questions that this ending poses: too many to be surveyed or discussed here. In the first chapter, I outlined a number of possibilities: the ending serves to discredit the disciples who represent a group in the community to which the implied author writes, who have a wrong understanding of Jesus (Theodore J. Weeden). Or, the ending demonstrates that the Jerusalem church was wrong in expecting the kingdom to appear in Jerusalem. Galilee is the place of the kingdom, a realm that will include both Jews and Gentiles (Werner H. Kelber). The ending projects a future meeting of the risen Jesus with his disciples. This will occur in Galilee, but beyond the end of the plotted story (Norman R. Petersen). I am inclined to follow Petersen in my reading of the ending, and so what follows is based upon his interpretation.

The message that the women receive from the young man in white includes the instruction to tell Jesus' disciples (including Peter) that he is going ahead of them to Galilee; there they will see him, *"just as he told you"* (16:7). These words recall 14:28, where Jesus, having predicted that the disciples would all abandon him, states that when he has been raised up, he will go before them to Galilee. The reader recalls that in this Gospel, as Petersen demonstrates, Jesus makes a number of predictions. Many of them are fulfilled within the story's "plotted time." There are, for instance, the passion predictions; and in this passage (14:27–28), Jesus predicts the desertion of the disciples, and the denials of Peter both of which subsequently occur. Hence the reader may expect that those predictions of Jesus that have not been fulfilled by the end of the narrative, will be fulfilled in "story time" beyond the end of the plotted story.

Thus the reader may imaginatively project a meeting of the disciples, with Jesus, beyond the story's end, when the disciples will be reinstated as faithful disciples. In fact, there is a feature of the Gospel's plot, namely, the inclusion of Mark 13 within plotted time, that reinforces this sense; but that is for the next chapter. In the meantime, the reader may accept that the disciples do receive the message delivered to the women that they are to go to Galilee where they will meet Jesus. They do go to Galilee: and they meet Jesus. And what is Galilee? Galilee is the place of Jesus' mission (and the disciples' mission) and it is the place where the disciples learned about discipleship, and what it means to follow Jesus. Galilee is the place of their beginning in discipleship, and the place of their future discipleship.

4

Mark 13
An "Embedded" End to the Gospel?

THE PLACE OF MARK 13 IN THE GOSPEL'S PLOT

THE THIRTEENTH CHAPTER OF Mark's Gospel seems to many readers to sit awkwardly in its present position. As Joel Marcus points out, there seems to be "a natural connection between the end of Mark 12 and the beginning of Mark 14," as a poor widow devotes her whole life to "the cause of God," and Jesus begins his journey of "God-willed sacrifice" to his death.[1] The story, it is felt, would flow much more smoothly without chapter 13. Many scholars have proposed different solutions to explain its presence here. It is a piece of tradition that has been included here: one suggestion is that it is an "apocalyptic flier," a pamphlet

---

1. Marcus, *Mark 8–16*, 864.

produced to give encouragement and hope to Christians in the face of the imminent siege of Jerusalem.[2]

Some regard this chapter as representing a "farewell discourse," that is, the final speech of someone about to die, who wishes to "warn the coming generation(s) of the trials they will face and exhort them to be faithful to God."[3] However this chapter may have been formed, or whatever the sources that may lie behind it, it is my contention that the implied author has placed it here for his own particular purposes, and that it is integral to the Gospel's story. We shall see how this is so as we proceed.

MARK 13 AND THE FIRST-CENTURY READER

Although there is little agreement on the precise details, scholars generally consider that this chapter gives us an insight into the situation of the first-century readers for whom this Gospel was written. This is, to a large degree, because of verse 14 where some actual person or event seems to be referred to and the importance of whom, or which, the implied author draws particular attention. The verse reads: "But when you see the desolating sacrilege set up where it ought not to be (let the reader understand), then those in Judea must flee to the mountains. . . ." It is the little aside by the narrator, "let the reader understand," that captures attention. It seems to suggest that "the reader" should sit up and pay particular attention at this point.

This narrative aside is itself not entirely straightforward. As twenty-first-century readers, we naturally assume that "the reader" is the first-century person who was reading

2. See here Collins, *Mark*, 596; and Taylor, *St. Mark*, 498.
3. Culpepper, *Mark*, 444.

Mark 13

the Gospel. But given that many first-century people would not have been able to read, and that this Gospel would most likely have been read aloud in a Christian assembly, this instruction might (must?) have been directed at the *reader* designated to read the text aloud to the listening congregation. The "lector" (to give a technical name to this person) then is to "understand" something at this point, perhaps with a view to giving the listeners some further clarification. But what exactly?

The most likely answer seems to be that the reader should understand something about "the desolating sacrilege." What might this be? The Greek here is somewhat difficult to interpret because it combines a neuter noun (Greek: *to bdelugma*, "the something detestable" [of desolation]) with a verb in the masculine case ("standing") that suggests a person, or a human *act*.[4] R. Alan Culpepper considers that the New English Bible (NEB) captures the sense well by rendering the verse, "when you see 'the abomination of desolation' usurping a place that is not *his*."[5]

The phrase itself, "the desolating sacrilege" (NRSV), or "the abomination of desolation" (NEB), comes from the book of Daniel (see Dan 9:27; 11:31; 12:11) where it appears to be connected to an interruption to, and replacement of, the regular temple worship. The reference in Daniel is understood to refer to the way in which Antiochus IV Epiphanes desecrated the temple in 168 BCE when he set up an altar dedicated to Zeus where the altar of burnt offering was and sacrificed a pig on it. He also outlawed the practice of Judaism.[6] Thus, his actions were an abomination to

---

4. Boring, *Mark*, 367; and Hooker, *Gospel According to Mark*, 314, who says that the writer may be "thinking of the person behind the symbol."

5. Culpepper, *Mark*, 459.

6. On this see Lane, *Gospel of Mark*, 466.

law-abiding Jews and brought "desolation" to their religious hopes and aspirations.

So, might the reference in Mark be to some incident in the temple, some act of desecration, or something that interrupted the temple worship? Two events have suggested themselves. In 40 CE the Emperor Caligula ordered his local representative, the imperial legate, to erect his statue in the temple. However, this incident does not seem the most likely referent as the order was eventually rescinded and Caligula was murdered soon after.[7] As the Jewish war in 66–70 CE wore on, the Jewish nationalist group took control of the temple and committed several objectionable acts, including carrying out murder within the temple precincts; and in the winter of 67/68 CE engaged in the farcical investiture of Phannias, a "mere rustic," as high priest.[8] The end of the temple came in 70 CE when the Roman general, Titus, after besieging Jerusalem, finally took it and, placing Roman standards in the temple area, was acclaimed *imperator*.[9]

Hence, for a number of commentators, some of the details of this chapter seem to fit the period of the Jewish war and they date the writing of the Gospel either to the period leading up to the fall of Jerusalem (say from the mid-sixties) or to just after the fall of Jerusalem in 70 CE. However, the details that can be gleaned from Mark 13 are vague, and some do not seem to fit the way that events actually unfolded, if the narrative is understood as having been written post-70 CE.

---

7. See Culpepper, *Mark*, 460.

8. Josephus, "Jewish War," bk. 4, ch. 3:8, in *New Complete Works of Josephus*, trans. Whiston, 813.

9. See the useful chronology of the Jewish war in Culpepper, *Mark*, 460.

Mark 13

Furthermore, much depends upon where the intended readers are thought to reside. Verses 14 to 18 would only make sense as a warning if readers were located in Judea and Galilee. If the warning was read after the event, it would have no practical relevance whatsoever. All things considered, it is probable that the message of this chapter is intended to have broad application to the lives of the readers, or hearers, even those of the later first century.

In this respect, there are three aspects that would apply widely to the lives of first-century Christians. One is the repeated warning to beware and to be on one's guard against "false Christs" and false messiahs (13:5b–6, 21–23) and false teachers generally. We know from the letters of Paul and the first epistle of John, for instance, that false teachers and prophets were a problem in the early church. Moreover, in the years around the beginning of the Christian era, and around the time of the Jewish war in particular, within the wider Jewish community there were a number of characters who arose and claimed to be, or were considered to be, a "messiah." Craig Evans lists the following: Judas, son of the "brigand chief" Hezekiah (4 BCE), Simon of Perea (4 BCE), Athronges, the shepherd of Judea (4–2 BCE), Menahem, son of Judas of Galilee (66 CE), Simon Bar-Giora (68–70 CE); and to these we might add Theudas (mentioned in Acts 5:36), an unnamed Egyptian false prophet, and John of Gischala (who operated during the time of the Jewish war).[10] So Christians would need to be reassured that "their Jesus" was the true Messiah, and encouraged to maintain belief in him in the face of any other supposed messiahs, or in a situation of unrest and unsettledness generally.

Second, there are warnings and exhortations to the disciples to be vigilant and unwavering in the face of

10. Evans, *Mark 8:27—16:20*, 360; and see the useful table in Culpepper, *Mark*, 450.

persecution and the likelihood of suffering at the hands of authorities for their faith. The book of Acts, not to mention hints in Revelation, and some personal testimony by Paul, as well as the experiences of later Christians, provide evidence of the range and types of persecution and opposition to which early Christians were subject. Following a fire in Rome, the Emperor Nero chose to make Christians the scapegoats for this, perhaps to deflect suspicion that he himself had something to do with its outbreak. Many were subjected to cruel deaths in the Roman arena. One scholar, Martin Hengel, though not entirely ready to associate the Gospel's depiction of Christians being "hated by all" with "[the] cruel events of 64 (CE)," nevertheless sees a fitting life setting for the Gospel's readers in the Neronian persecution.[11] So, if the readers were Roman Christians as some think, then such a Gospel written around the time of the persecution or soon after would serve as a reminder that endurance in the face of suffering was required of Christians (Mark 13:13).

However, and as a third point, the writer is at pains to moderate expectations of the *Parousia*. Again, we know that expectations were high among numbers of Christians in the first century. The writer thus provides a number of statements which would damp down expectations of an imminent *Parousia*. Though there may be wars and rumors of war, the end is still to come (13:7). These, or natural disasters such as earthquakes and famines, are "but the beginning of the birth pangs" (13:8). Indeed, even in the face of persecution and suffering, and perhaps even by means of these, "the good news must first be proclaimed to all nations" (13:10). This, if anything, should give readers reason to expect that the end might be some time off.

---

11. See Hengel, *Studies*, 23–24; cf. Culpepper, *Mark*, 458.

Mark 13

Furthermore, even as one must remain watchful and ready for the return of the Master, it is important to remember that no one, not even "the Son," knows the precise day or hour: that is, privileged information known only by "the Father" (13:32). I suggest, then, that even for the original readers, the message of this chapter was an enduring one whatever their circumstances: be alert, remain faithful. While they may have understood particular details as pertinent to actual events and matters of their lives, it is impossible for modern readers at this distance to be certain what these were. Nevertheless, these admonitions remain enduring in their application. The teaching may be represented as private teaching given to four named disciples, but it is intended for all disciples and all readers (or hearers).

MARK 13 AND THE END OF "STORY TIME"

You will recall the distinction made by Norman R. Petersen between "story time" and "plotted time." "Plotted time" refers to the chronological progress of the story as arranged by the implied author. "Story time" refers to the overall chronology of time assumed by the events narrated or referred to in the plot. That is, the beginning point and the end point of the story as suggested by the events narrated. We saw that the story in Mark's Gospel begins with the preaching of John the Baptist (though in the quotation from Isaiah that the implied author provides a prior event is in view, namely, the time that the prophecy was made).

We have seen that the implied author ends the story abruptly at 16:8 with the statement that the women run away from the tomb and say nothing to anyone because they are afraid. But the words of the young man (16:7) project another event which will happen sometime in the proximate future, namely, that when the disciples go to Galilee they will meet Jesus there (this reiterates what Jesus had already told the disciples, see 14:28). In Mark chapter 13, in some teaching by Jesus, we learn of more events, which will happen sometime in the future. This future, and the times when these events will occur, is somewhat indeterminate; but the reader assumes (and must assume on the basis of what is said) that these events will happen at a time after the death and resurrection of Jesus, the Son of Man.

The events spoken of in Mark 13, then, occur after the end of the plotted story time. As they appear in the discourse of Jesus prior to his death, and refer to events that will happen beyond the end of the plotted story time, we receive them not only as anticipations of events that will happen in the future, but as events that are plotted out of time, as it were. They are extensions of story time into the future. They represent events, if you will, that will happen beyond the end of the plotted story time but have been placed back into "plotted time." The diagram below may help illustrate this process.

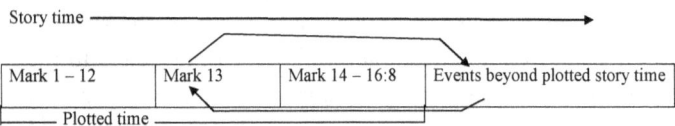

Figure 1

JESUS' TEACHING IN MARK 13

Jesus and the disciples depart the temple, where Jesus has been engaged in debates with the authorities and answering the questions posed by various groups and people before posing a significant question about the Messiah himself. In company with the disciples, Jesus has just observed and commented upon a poor widow contributing to the temple treasury "everything she had, all she had to live on." As they

Mark 13

depart, one of the disciples comments on the magnificence of the buildings, and the large stones used to construct them. This prompts Jesus to state that one day the temple will be destroyed, with "not one stone left . . . upon another" (13:2).

This statement of Jesus prompts a question from some of the disciples about when "these things" will take place. Jesus embarks on some extended teaching (the second piece of extended teaching after that of Mark 4). It is important to notice some features of the way in which this teaching is introduced. First, it is delivered as Jesus is seated on the Mount of Olives, over against the temple. From a vantage point anywhere on the Mount of Olives, the temple would dominate the view of Jerusalem. The Mount of Olives was an appropriate place for Jesus to deliver teaching that suggested the coming of the kingdom of God. The phrasing in Mark 13:3 recalls that found in Zechariah 14:4, and in Zechariah 14:4–5 the Mount of Olives is identified as the place where the Lord will stand after defeating Israel's enemies. From there the reign of God over the whole earth will be inaugurated.[12] In the writer's understanding of the Old Testament, "the Mount of Olives," says M. Eugene Boring, "had apocalyptic overtones."[13] Jesus takes up the posture of a teacher: particularly that of a rabbi teaching his disciples.

The teaching that takes place is a "private seminar." It is teaching given to four disciples only. These are named as Peter, James, John, and Andrew. The reader will recall that these are the four disciples first called by Jesus right at the outset of Jesus' time in Galilee. Scholars note that the order in which they are named is different, however, as Andrew is named last, separated from that of his brother

12. On this see Hooker, *Gospel According to Mark*, 305, and Marcus, *Mark 8–16*, 869; see also Culpepper, *Mark*, 447.

13. Boring, *Mark*, 354.

by the names of the other two brothers, James and John. The order they are named is that in which they are listed when Jesus appoints the twelve apostles (see Mark 3:13–19, especially vv. 16–18a). But, more to the point, is the fact that by this stage in the Gospel's story, Peter, James, and John have emerged as a triumvirate forming a kind of "inner core" of Jesus' disciples. They, alone of all the disciples, went with Jesus to the house of Jairus, when Jesus raised his daughter to life (see 5:37). They were with Jesus on the Mount of Transfiguration (as it is conventionally called; see Mark 9:2), and engaged with Jesus on the question of the coming of Elijah (9:9–13). Furthermore, there is a sense in which they have been particularly singled out as struggling with the concept of messiahship and discipleship that Jesus has put forth (see Mark 8:29–33; 9:38–41; 10:35–45). We shall see that they most spectacularly and thoroughly fail to heed some of the most important teaching Jesus delivers to them in this chapter. I do not believe that the order of the disciples' names is anything but a deliberate strategy on the part of the implied author. Moreover, these four disciples, the four first called, receive this teaching as representatives of all the disciples.

The teaching in this chapter has to do both with events that will happen in the future generally; and specifically with events and circumstances that the disciples will face. In this latter regard, this chapter may be seen as confirming the fulfillment of Jesus' promise and the young man's prediction that when the disciples go to Galilee after Jesus has been raised up, they will meet Jesus and they will be rehabilitated and reinstated as Jesus' faithful disciples. The reader may be sure of this for the chapter speaks about the testimony that the disciples will bear, and how they will be beaten in the synagogue, and stand before governors and kings on account of their allegiance to Jesus (13:9). So, in

Mark 13

this respect, the reader may in retrospect understand Mark 13 as providing another end to the Gospel. It is an end "embedded" in the Gospel's "plotted time," and tells the reader of the eventual fate of the disciples. The narrator's comment at 14:50, that the disciples "all deserted him and fled"; or the picture of Peter at the conclusion of that same chapter breaking down and weeping because he has denied Jesus three times, as Jesus said he would, is not the last word on these disciples. In chapter 13, the reader has it from the lips of Jesus himself that they will bear witness to him.

So, in this chapter, the reader gains an insight into the life of the disciples after the resurrection, and also receives information about the end of Jerusalem, and the end of this world itself. The reader will discover, too, that again there is a "turn to the reader" so that he or she is drawn into the story and may understand Jesus' words as directed at him- or herself. We shall look at each of these aspects in turn.

Why would the implied author have chosen to place this chapter here? I suggest that it is not only because Jesus has just been in the temple, but also because at this point in the Gospel's plot the time of Jesus' ministry is drawing to a close. Chapter 14 will begin the "passion narrative": the story of Jesus' own progress toward death, when he will take up his cross in fulfillment of his role as the servant-king, who came "not to be served but to serve, and to give his life a ransom for many" (10:45). Moreover, the previous chapter has concluded with the story of the widow who has contributed her all to the temple treasury, the same temple that Jesus declared a "den of robbers" (11:17b), and now, at the outset of chapter 13, prophecies its destruction. This prophecy leads directly into Jesus' foreshadowing the life of the disciples in the future: a life that will call for sacrifice and the giving of one's all.

THE LIFE OF THE DISCIPLES AFTER THE RESURRECTION

"Tell us," the four disciples ask, "when will this be, and what will be the sign that all these things are about to be accomplished?" (13:4). Reading Mark 13 is a little bit like looking at a range of hills and mountains along the horizon. From the perspective of some distance away, the hills and mountains lie "flat" along the horizon as it were. But when one gets closer, perhaps into the hills, one realizes that what looked from a distance to be standing all along one line, is, in fact, separated by valleys in between. Or, we might imagine a range of hills behind which lies a broad, open plain before the terrain begins to lift again into a further range of foothills and mountains.

So it is with this chapter: it is difficult to tell when the events that Jesus speaks about will happen, and whether they will occur all at about the same time or not. Will all the events Jesus refers to occur within the lifetime of the disciples, or will some of them fall outside the lives of the disciples? In fact, from our vantage point as twenty-first-century readers, we may surmise that some of the events written about here took place in the lives of the disciples, or, at least, if taken to refer to events that had happened or were about to happen when the Gospel was written, then in the lives of first-century readers of the Gospel. We explored some of the possible historical circumstances to which this chapter may refer above.

Jesus issues a number of warnings to the disciples. First, they are to be aware (and beware!) that there will be false teachers, and people appearing who claim to be the Messiah, or who think someone else is. "Many will come in my name," says Jesus, "and say, 'I am he!' and they will lead many astray" (13:6). And again, "If anyone says to you

Mark 13

at that time, 'Look! Here is the Messiah!' or 'Look! There he is!'—do not believe it. False messiahs and false prophets will appear and produce signs and omens, to lead astray, if possible, the elect" (13:21–22).

Next, they are to realize that they themselves will be subject to troubles and persecution. They will be put on trial, made to answer to "councils" (probably to be understood as the ruling bodies of synagogues) and beaten in synagogues. They will stand to give testimony or witness before governors and kings. In the face of this, they should not worry about what they will say in their defense, for when the time comes the Holy Spirit will enable them to find the words. But the severest test will be the fact that families will be split. Family members will bring about the death of siblings, children, or parents as they testify against them, or ensure that they are handed over to the authorities. The disciples will find themselves hated "by all" on account of Jesus. This will call for courage and endurance. In a statement reminiscent of the exhortations found in the book of Revelation, Jesus states that "the one who endures to the end will be saved" (13:13b).

Finally, they are to be ready for the eventualities of crisis and a time of suffering. One period of crisis appears to be quite specific and localized: it is when "the abomination of desolation" is seen to be "set up where it ought not to be." This then is a time for those in Judea to take action: basically to flee. The other time is an unknown time when the Son of Man will come, and angels will go out to the four corners of the earth to gather in "his elect." This can only be prepared for by constant vigilance, and by faithful execution of one's allotted duties.

That these words are directed at the disciples and their situation is confirmed by a number of textual and verbal signals. There is the continual use of the second person plural, "you." There are the repeated exhortations to "beware" and to pay heed. One particularly clear indication is the statement in 13:23 that the disciples have already been told everything, and so, the inference is, they are forewarned and hence forearmed.

THE END IN JUDEA AND THE END OF THE WORLD

As noted above, Mark 13 appears to have two timeframes in view. One is a timeframe that relates to events that will take place in Judea. This is signaled most clearly in verse 14 where Jesus says that when the disciples observe "the desolating sacrilege" set up where it should not be "then those in Judea must flee to the mountains."[14] This is a time of crisis where speed of departure is of the essence: one should not delay to pick up any belongings, nor, if one is away from home, return there to collect one's coat. Mercifully, this will be a time of short, if intense, suffering: Jesus says one should pray that it does not happen in winter. All this suggests a local and well-defined event. But it is one that is difficult to identify now, though the period of the Jewish war offers a plausible timeframe.

The other timeframe is less determinate. It has to do with "the end" and it will culminate with "the Son of Man coming in the clouds" (13:26). This is the time generally known as the *Parousia*, the time of the appearing of the Son of Man, or the Messiah, and in much modern parlance

14. Commentators puzzle over this statement, noting that Jerusalem itself (from which presumably people should be fleeing) is on a mountain amidst mountains. They debate which mountains might be meant. But this is to misunderstand a statement that is meant to be taken figuratively: it is like the saying, "Head for the hills!"; or to put it in other colloquial terms, "Get out of here!"

Mark 13

associated with "the end of the world," or "the Second Coming of Jesus."[15] In his discourse, Jesus' gaze is largely fixed on this longer, indeterminate timeframe, even though the initial exchange about the temple which sparks the four disciples' question about the timing of events probably is to be associated with the destruction of the temple in 70 CE.

While the focus eventually brings the *Parousia* into view, Jesus is concerned also to warn that there will be an intermediate period when the disciples must beware lest they be led astray by false prophets and messiahs, and when they must be prepared to take their stand and witness in religious and "secular" courts: or to put it differently, to appear before Jewish and pagan authorities. Furthermore, events such as wars, earthquakes, and famines will occur, and the gospel will spread throughout the nations before the end comes.

When the end does come, there will be dramatic signs aplenty. The lights of heaven will go out and "the powers in the heavens will be shaken" (13:24). This will be the time when the Son of Man appears in great power and glory and when the elect will be gathered in from "the four winds" (all corners of the earth), and, indeed, from all parts of the universe. The language used here is typical of apocalyptic language, and very evocative of Old Testament language about "the day of the Lord" or the appearing of God in judgment (see, for instance, among other texts, Isa 13:10, cf. 34:4; Zeph 1:15; Joel 2:10; 3:15).[16] This language is not to

15. Apart from talking about the *Parousia*, or the Messiah's "appearing," it is probably better, I think, to avoid "end of world" and "second coming" language for Mark's understanding, as these concepts have gathered so much around them drawn from interpretations based on other parts of the New Testament, not to mention modern speculation.

16. On the evocation of Old Testament language, and further examples, see Evans, *Mark 8:27—16:20*, 327, and Hooker, *Gospel*

be taken literally, I think, but it is to be understood as designating the climactic and definitive nature of this end. It will be the time when the Son of Man's authority will be finally and fully established, and when he will come in power to enact judgment and the vindication of "the elect."

Not only is this time indeterminate, but it is not even to be determined. Though it is preceded by recurrent and ongoing disasters (wars, earthquakes, famines), though "worldwide evangelization" continues in the lead up to it, and though it is inaugurated with dramatic cosmic signs, no one, not even the Son, knows its precise date or time. This is privileged information known only to "the Father." The only preparation possible, or even necessary, is simply to be vigilant and faithful in doing one's appointed tasks, and fulfilling one's allotted role.

THE LESSON OF THE FIG TREE

Jesus puts forward a visual aid as a way of helping the disciples to know when the Son of Man will come. When the fig tree puts out new shoots and leaves begin to sprout, then one knows that summer is on its way. So there will be signs, like the shoots and leaves on the fig tree, that will signal the time is near. But the reader, who has read the story to this point, also knows that Jesus can appear looking for fruit on a fig tree out of season. In that case, the end of the fig tree came "at the word of the Lord," quite unexpectedly. So,

---

According to Mark, 318. Note that some texts have in view the judgment of God upon Israel or Judah which was achieved in events of military defeat or the experience of occupation and exile; or God's action against Israel's oppressors (e.g. Isa 13:10, which "concerns the destruction of Babylon," see Evans, *Mark 8:27–16:20*, 328). Thus, as with Jesus' discourse in Mark 13, not all such language need designate the events of "the end of the world."

Mark 13

perhaps the reader should not be surprised to find that Jesus says that no one knows the "when" of "that day or hour" (meaning the time of the Son of Man's coming). This is in the hands of the Father, who, like the master of a house (to change the metaphor), having gone on a journey, returns suddenly at an unexpected hour. The only way to truly be ready is to be ever vigilant: to "keep awake."

"KEEP AWAKE": THE TURN TO THE READER

In terms of "plotted time," Jesus' words to the disciples in 13:33–36 will come to have a particularly ironic ring to them. Here they are warned to be aware for they do not know when the time will come. They are enjoined to keep awake, for they may be suddenly overtaken by events. And sure enough: they do find themselves in a situation where, failing to be alert and awake, they are overtaken by events. The reader discovers that when Jesus arrives at the garden of Gethsemane on the night of his arrest, he again selects Peter, James and John to go with him to a place apart from the other disciples where he wishes to pray. In fact, he confesses to being in a state of mortal distress, and asks these three to "remain here, and keep awake." Meanwhile, he goes a little farther off and begins to pray earnestly that he may be spared the coming ordeal. But, in any event, he will fulfill his Father's will. When he returns to the three disciples, he finds them all sleeping. Addressing them all, through Simon, he asks whether they are not able to remain awake. He repeats the command, "Keep awake and pray that you may not come into the time of trial" (14:38).[17] Vigilance against

17. The parable of the master of the house going on a journey spells out the times that the master may return as being "in the evening, or at midnight, or at cockcrow, or at dawn" (13:35). We might

the "time of trial," and in the face of "the hour," is something that the disciples are exhorted to do in Jesus' teaching in Mark chapter 13. The circumstance of Jesus finding the disciples asleep occurs three times. On the third occasion Jesus announces, "Enough! The hour has come..." (14:41). It is shortly after this that these three, along with the others, desert Jesus and flee. Peter will subsequently attempt to follow Jesus, at a distance, but will finally find himself denying Jesus.

But Jesus' final word in Mark chapter thirteen is not just directed at the four disciples involved in this "private seminar." In Mark 13:37, Jesus says, "And what I say to you I say to all: Keep awake." Who are these all? Perhaps, the "all" are all the other disciples who are not privy to this teaching. Perhaps, the "all" are all the other characters in the story: or at least, that penumbra of people ("the crowd," "those around him") who with the disciples are invited to take up the challenge of discipleship. I suggest that the "all" is also every reader of this Gospel. In that case, the teaching of Jesus in this chapter is pertinent to all readers in all ages. Even though readers may not be able to relate to the events that are said to happen in Judea, they are potentially included in other aspects of this chapter's events. They, too, will hear of wars and rumors of wars. They experience situations of conflict and they experience or hear of earthquakes and famines. Many know of persecution, and betrayal by family. And every generation still looks for that unknown day, not able to be timetabled, when the kingdom of God and of the

---

imagine that in the story as it subsequently unfolds, it is "in the evening" when Jesus asks the three disciples to watch in prayer, "midnight" when Jesus is arrested and the disciples all flee, "at cockcrow" when Peter denies Jesus, and "at dawn" when Jesus is put on trial before Pilate, by which time all the disciples have gone into hiding. Mark 13, then, contains an ironic hint of developments that will be fulfilled within story time.

Mark 13

Son of Man will be fully established. Above all, they hear, and must heed, the exhortation: Keep awake! And, when this chapter is read as the end of the Gospel's story time, then it is found to end in a way that is every bit as open-ended as the ending of the Gospel's plotted time.

Epilogue
Reading Mark's Gospel

THE PRECEDING CHAPTERS HAVE given you a reading of Mark's Gospel. This is one of many possible readings of the Gospel. Others have read this Gospel under the impetus of exploring other themes and questions; although the themes of Jesus' identity and discipleship (which I have covered in the book) appear in many studies of the Gospel. Now, my reading is not a full reading of the Gospel. My interest, in addition to exploring the themes mentioned above, has been to attempt to show you some of the interconnections within the Gospel, and to outline some of the implied author's "tricks of his trade." I have also read the Gospel under the impress of the question of Mark's ending: and I have suggested to you that its "open" ending (at 16:8) provides opportunities for interesting readings of the Gospel.

Above all, I hope that this book stimulates you to continue to explore the Gospel for yourself. What do you make of its ending? How do you understand the issues and themes, and the questions that the story throws up? What follows is a series of studies and sets of study questions that I have used with groups on previous occasions to open up

Epilogue: Reading Mark's Gospel

the Gospel. You might like to use them, either as an individual or with a group, to help you explore the Gospel. A good exercise, before you start, is to read the Gospel through at one sitting so that you get a sense of the whole story.

As the questions which follow have been based on the New Revised Standard Version of the Bible (NRSV), you may find it helpful to use that version in consulting the text of Mark. That is not to say that other versions may not be used: and most questions, no doubt, will make perfect sense whatever version is being consulted. But should you find a question that does not make sense when applied to another version, try the NRSV.

STUDY 1: WHO IS THIS MAN?

Read Mark 1:1–14

1. What does the reader learn about Jesus from verse 1?[1]
2. What does the reader learn about Jesus from what John the Baptist says, and from the story of the baptism?
3. Mark 1:11 seems to combine a quotation (and ideas) from Psalm 2:7 with Isaiah 42:1. Psalm 2 is a "royal psalm" that speaks about God's relationship with, and care for, the king of Israel.

    a. Read Psalm 2:7: What does reference to this verse by Mark suggest for his understanding of Jesus' role?

    b. Read Isaiah 42:1: Who is addressed in this verse? What does this suggest about Jesus' role? If we put the description of Jesus suggested by using Psalm 2:7, with the description suggested by Isaiah 42:1,

---

1. In what follows, "v." means "verse; "vv." means "verses".

Epilogue: Reading Mark's Gospel

what do we get?

4. According to Mark 1:14, when does Jesus begin his ministry? What does this suggest about John's preaching and baptizing ministry and Jesus' ministry?

Read Mark 1:21–28

1. What does the evil spirit in the man cry out?
2. Why does Jesus silence the man (compare 1:34 and 3:11–12)?
3. What is the reaction of the crowd who witness this exorcism (the casting out of the evil spirit)?

Read Mark 2:1–12

Notice that already Jesus' ministry is so successful and widespread, and he is so popular, that he is speaking to "sell-out" crowds (see 1:28, 32–33, 37, 39 ["throughout Galilee"], 45).

1. What is your answer to Jesus' question in verse 9? Why?
2. By making the paralyzed man stand up, what else (besides healing him) is Jesus doing for the man? What does this action demonstrate to the scribes and the crowd that he has authority to do?
3. If "only God can forgive sins" (see v. 7), what does Jesus' healing of the paralyzed man suggest about who Jesus is?
4. What is the reaction of the crowd?

Epilogue: Reading Mark's Gospel

Read Mark 4:35–41

1. What is the disciples' reaction to Jesus' calming of the storm?

2. Read Psalm 107:23–30: This psalm is about deliverance by God from the stormy sea. Imagine that the disciples remembered this psalm when they saw Jesus stilling the storm. What possible answer to their question (in v. 41) might the psalm suggest to them?

Read Mark 8:27–33

1. In verse 27, Jesus asks his disciples, "Who do people say that I am?" What answers do they give him?

2. Why do people think that Jesus is John the Baptist or Elijah? (One person who thinks Jesus is John the Baptist is Herod; see 6:14–15).

3. What is the significance of Elijah (see Mark 9:11–13)?

4. What other titles or descriptions of Jesus might people now be expected to offer, having seen what he can do?

5. What answer does Peter give to the question of who Jesus is? Is he right?

6. Why does Peter rebuke Jesus (in v. 32)? What does he not like about what Jesus is saying?

7. Why does Jesus rebuke Peter (in v. 33)? What is wrong with Peter's thinking?

8. If you were to construct a "profile" of Jesus at this point in your reading of the Gospel, what would you say about Jesus?

Epilogue: Reading Mark's Gospel

STUDY 2: INSIDERS OR OUTSIDERS?

Read Mark 1:16–20

1. Who are called to be Jesus' disciples? How does the story indicate that they are being called to be disciples?
2. How do they respond to Jesus' call?
3. What do they leave behind?

Read Mark 2:13–17

1. What does Levi leave in order to follow Jesus?
2. What does this passage tell us about what qualifies one to be part of Jesus' company?
3. Note verse 15b ("many followed him," and compare 3:7). Are all who follow Jesus necessarily disciples?

Read Mark 3:31–35

1. Where are Jesus' mother and brothers when they ask for him?
2. To whom does Jesus speak?
3. What defines those whom Jesus says are his mother and brothers?
4. What effect does this episode have upon the reader's understanding of "Jesus' family"?

Epilogue: Reading Mark's Gospel

Read Mark 4:1–20

1. According to Jesus in verses 10–11, to whom has the secret (or "mystery") of the kingdom of God been given (i.e., to whom does "you" refer)?

2. Jesus quotes, or adapts, Isaiah 6:9–10 (see v. 12) to describe those who are "outside." What, according to verse 12, are the characteristics of those who do not understand? How should this be understood: *literally* (so that the parables are told deliberately to made people unable to understand), or *ironically and symbolically*, so that the quotation means, in effect, "if only they would be prepared to truly see and hear, they would understand and be forgiven"?[2]

3. Who are "those outside" referred to in verse 11? (See also 3:31–35: Is there supposed to be a connection here?) Can we divide those who are in contact with Jesus into "insiders" and "outsiders"?

4. The disciples are described as "insiders": they have been given the secret of the kingdom of God. But they don't understand the parable. Where does this place them?

5. What are some of the reasons given in Mark 4:15–18 as to why people fail to accept, or receive, "the word"?

Read Mark 6:30–44

The apostles (or disciples) report back on a mission that Jesus has sent them out on (see 6:7–13).

1. What are some of the things that they have done?

---

[2]. You might also like to compare how Matthew treats this quotation of Isaiah; see Matt 13:10–15. Note also Mark 4:24–25.

Epilogue: Reading Mark's Gospel

2. Jesus takes the disciples away for some "rest and recreation" after their mission, but they are followed by crowds whom Jesus teaches. When it is getting late, the disciples want Jesus to send the crowds away to buy food. Why does Jesus ask the disciples to themselves give the crowd something to eat? Should they have been able to oblige?

3. If this feeding miracle takes place in Jewish territory (and is a continuation of the disciples' mission), what is the significance of the fact that twelve baskets of leftovers are collected up? What do these stand for?

Read Mark 6:45–52

1. In verse 52, why does Mark say that "they were utterly astounded [when Jesus joined them in the boat and stilled the storm] for they did not understand *about the loaves*"? What does the miracle of the loaves, or the feeding of the five thousand, have to do with this situation?

2. "For their hearts were hardened" (v. 52b). Of what does this statement remind you?

Read Mark 8:1–9

1. This miracle (the feeding of four thousand people) takes place in Gentile territory (in the region of Decapolis; see Mark 7:31). On the occasion of this second feeding miracle, Jesus takes the initiative and suggests (the story implies this) that he will feed the crowd. Should the disciples have had to ask how this would be done (see v. 4)?

Epilogue: Reading Mark's Gospel

2. Jesus gets the disciples to distribute the bread (after he has given thanks, v. 6).[3] Is there any significance in the fact that there are seven baskets of leftovers? What might this fact stand for?

Read Mark 8:11–21

1. How much bread do the disciples have with them?

2. What do you think is meant by the "yeast" of the Pharisees and of Herod?

3. Why do the disciples worry about having no bread (v. 16)? Should they?

4. Read verses 17–18: What do Jesus' words here remind you of? Where, before this passage, have we read of eyes that fail to see and ears that fail to hear? What does this suggest about the disciples?

5. Read verse 21: What should the disciples understand?

6. What is the answer to Jesus' question in verse 21? Do the disciples understand?

---

3. Note that the word in the Greek for "giving thanks" is *eucharistein* (here, *eucharistēsas*, "he gave thanks") from which we get our word, "Eucharist" (the name given in some churches to the service of Holy Communion). In Mark 6:7 it says that before Jesus got the disciples to distribute some fish, he blessed the fish. Both these words, "to give thanks" and "to bless," are used in Mark 14:22–26 in the story of the institution of the Lord's Supper. Thus Mark the storyteller is creating a link between this feeding story and the story of the institution of the Lord's Supper. Both the feeding of the five thousand and of the four thousand take place in "deserted" places. This perhaps reminds readers familiar with the Old Testament that God fed the people of Israel in the wilderness. The great amounts of food created perhaps taps into Jewish belief that in the messianic age there would be plenty to eat and great banquets, even in wilderness places.

Epilogue: Reading Mark's Gospel

7. What is the effect of having no answer (from the disciples) to this question?

8. If no answer is given in the text, to whom might the question *also* be directed?

9. What do you think are the characteristics needed to be a disciple? Think back on the passages you have read and make a list of what you think are the characteristics of discipleship suggested by these.

STUDY 3: BEING A LEARNER-DISCIPLE

Read Mark 8:27–38

1. Is Peter correct when he identifies Jesus as "the Christ"?

2. What is Peter's reaction to what Jesus says about the Son of Man (see vv. 31–32)?

3. Why do you think Peter reacted in this way?

4. What is Jesus' reaction to Peter's rebuke?

5. Why is Peter said to be setting his mind on "human things" not on "divine things," or on the side of humans, not of God (RSV)?

6. What characteristics of discipleship does Jesus highlight in verses 34–38?

Read Mark 9:30–37

1. What is the disciples' reaction to Jesus' words in verses 31–32?

2. How does Jesus counter their argument about who is

Epilogue: Reading Mark's Gospel

the greatest?

3. What is the significance of using "a little child" to make his point?

Read Mark 10:46–52

1. How does Jesus' prediction of his passion in verses 32–34 differ from the previous ones (see 8:31; 9:31)?
2. What is the disciples' reaction to this teaching?
3. How does Jesus counter this attitude?
4. For each of these passages (8:31—9:1; 9:30–37; 10:32–45) note the following:
   a. What Jesus predicts about the future.
   b. How the disciples react and/or what they do next.
   c. What Jesus teaches about discipleship.
5. Can you detect a pattern in all three of these passages?
6. Over the course of this part of the story (from 8:27 to 10:45) what progress toward a better understanding of what it means to be a disciple do you think the disciples have made?

Read Mark 8:22–26 and Mark 10:46–52

Here are two stories that tell about the healing of a blind man. They stand as "bookends" to Mark 8:27—10:45.

1. In the first story (8:22–26) how is the blind man healed?
2. Why does the healing take place in two stages?
3. This is the only healing miracle that Jesus performs

Epilogue: Reading Mark's Gospel

where he has to make two attempts at healing the person. Why do you think this is so?

4. In the second story (10:46–52), the blind man is given a name, Bartimaeus, which means "son of Timaeus." Do you think there is any significance in the fact that we are told his name? What might this be?

5. What does Bartimaeus do when he hears that Jesus is passing by?

6. What does Bartimaeus call Jesus? What is the significance of this?

7. What does Jesus do? And what does he ask Bartimaeus?

8. What does Bartimaeus do in response to Jesus' call?

9. How does the way Bartimaeus receives his sight differ from the healing of the other blind man?

10. What does Bartimaeus do once his sight has been regained?

11. Where is Jesus headed when he heals Bartimaeus?

12. What indications are there in the story that Bartimaeus becomes a disciple of Jesus?

13. How are Bartimaeus' actions like that of the four disciples in Mark 1:16–20?

14. How are his actions different from the way their story unfolds?

STUDY 4: A SURPRISING ENDING

Read Mark 14:26–31

1. Jesus predicts that all the disciples will desert him (v. 27) and that Peter will deny him (v. 30). Do his

Epilogue: Reading Mark's Gospel

predictions come true? How?

2. See Mark 14:1–2, 10–11, 43–42, 66–72.

   a. What are the various ways in which the disciples fail?

   b. What is the significance of the story of the young man (14:51–52)?

3. What will Jesus do after he has been raised from the dead?

4. What is Peter's reaction to Jesus' prediction that he will desert and deny Jesus? What about the other disciples?

Read Mark 15:40—16:8[4]

1. How are the women described in 15:40–41? Should they be regarded as disciples?

    What role do they play in the story of the burial and resurrection of Jesus?

2. How is the news of Jesus' resurrection conveyed in the story?

3. What does the young man say will happen in Galilee? How is the reader reminded of Mark 14:28? Should we expect this prediction of Jesus, and the young man, to come true? What indications in the story help confirm this?

4. Why does the young man single out Peter for special mention?

5. Do the women fulfill their commission to tell the

---

4. For the purposes of this study, assume that Mark 16:8 is the original ending of the Gospel. For discussion of this, see chapter 1 of this book.

Epilogue: Reading Mark's Gospel

disciples the young man's message?

6. Why do you think that the story says that the women run away and don't say anything to anyone?

7. What is the effect of this ending?

8. What does "Galilee" stand for, or represent, in this Gospel? See, for example, Mark 1:14–20, 39.

9. Do you think that the Gospel implies that the disciples are eventually reunited with Jesus in Galilee? If so, how does it do this? If not, why not?

STUDY 5: "KEEP AWAKE": REMAINING A DISCIPLE

Read Mark 13

1. Who is the audience for Jesus' talk about the "end times" in this chapter?

2. When are the events of this chapter to take place?

3. What will be the experience of the disciples in the world in the time to which this chapter refers?

4. What do you think is meant by "the desolating sacrilege," or "the abomination that causes desolation" (NIV) that is set up "where it ought not to be" (v. 14)?

5. What are some of the attitudes that disciples must have and actions that they must take, according to this chapter?

6. What clues are there in this chapter that this talk of Jesus is meant for the time when the Gospel was written?

7. If this chapter gives some clues to the experience

Epilogue: Reading Mark's Gospel

of Christians at the time that the Gospel was written, what were some of the things that they were experiencing?

8. Do you think that readers are supposed to know the time of the end, or not?
9. When Jesus says, "What I say to *you* I say to *all*" (v. 37), who are the "you" and who are the "all"?
10. Is this chapter relevant to us today? If so, how?

Some Suggested Reading on Mark's Gospel

My own reading of Mark's Gospel has been informed and enriched by the scholarship of others. My hope, in part, for this book is that you will be enticed into exploring some of that scholarship. Here I provide a brief annotated reading list of books that I think will provide you with a good entrée to scholarship on the Gospel. In particular, at least three of them provide a reading that gives a literary reading of the Gospel, and one of them consciously uses the approach of narrative criticism, which has informed my own work.

Hooker, Morna D. *The Message of Mark*. London: Epworth, 1983.

Although this is an older book, it provides a straightforward, clear introduction to many of the issues of the Gospel, especially touching upon some older, more traditional scholarship. The book is based on a series of lectures, the heart of which being an examination of the Christology of the Gospel. Hooker writes in a forthright manner, on occasion taking issue with other scholars' readings, but she is always full of insight and wisdom.

Some Suggested Reading on Mark's Gospel

Juel, Donald H. *A Master of Surprise: Mark Interpreted.* Minneapolis: Fortress, 1994.

A delightful examination of the Gospel, delightful for its close reading of the narrative that notices links and interweavings in the story, and how earlier parts prepare for later. There is also an insightful and enthralling exposition of Markan themes. It is not a straightforward read, however, and you must persevere through to part 2, where he begins his own reading. Part 1 lays down an important argument for reading the Gospel as a connected narrative.

Kelber, Werner H. *Mark's Story of Jesus.* Philadelphia: Fortress, 1979.

This book is an early example of a literary reading of the Gospel that approaches the Gospel as "a dramatically plotted journey of Jesus." It works through the Gospel sequentially, showing how the motif of journey brings out themes of the Gospel.

Moloney, Francis J. *Mark: Storyteller, Interpreter, Evangelist.* Peabody: Hendrickson, 2004.

An introduction to the Gospel that is more detailed and technical than Hooker. This book covers all the major issues in interpretation. The section on "Storyteller" provides an overview of the Gospel's plot, dividing the text up into blocks of material, analyzing each in a mix of summary of the content and discussion of the techniques used to get the message across.

Rhoads, David, Joanna Dewey, and Donald Michie. *Mark as Story: An Introduction to the Narrative of a Gospel.* 3rd ed. Minneapolis: Fortress, 2012.

Some Suggested Reading on Mark's Gospel

This book provides a reading of the Gospel: the entire text of the Gospel appears as chapter 1, "set out as a short story," translated from the Greek by the authors. The book provides a literary analysis of the Gospel using the methods, or the approach, of narrative criticism, so that the book deals with the way the story is told, its settings, plot, and characters. Finally, the authors attend to the reader: both the "ideal reader" and putative first-century readers. This book is well worth reading for the insight it gives into reading the Gospel as a story.

This third edition adds to the second edition (1997) a preface that, among other matters, focuses on the Gospel as an "oral/aural composition." It also includes an afterword by Mark Allan Powell that discusses the impact on Markan scholarship of the first two editions of *Mark as Story*. Both the second and third editions contain a couple of appendices that help the reader analyze the narrative and learn and tell the story. This book is something of a classic, and you will profit from a reading of it irrespective of which edition you read.

Van Iersel, Bas. *Reading Mark*. Translated by W. H. Bisscheroux. Edinburgh: T. & T. Clark, 1989.

Like *Mark as Story*, this book gives a literary analysis of the Gospel, but works sequentially through the Gospel providing analysis of, and commentary on, the text. This Dutch scholar provides a stimulating and enlightening commentary, and some of his suggestions about the technique of parallels between stories are illuminating. He provides a close reading of the Gospel by examining the text under various topics, which means that understanding of the story is built up in a cumulative fashion, as well as sequentially. At times he brings in Old Testament (or, as he calls it, First Testament) texts to inform aspects of the Gospel. The

Some Suggested Reading on Mark's Gospel

book includes the entire text of the Gospel based on the New English Bible.

Bibliography

Boring, M. Eugene. *Mark: A Commentary*. New Testament Library. Louisville: Westminster John Knox, 2006.

Broadhead, Edwin K. *Naming Jesus: Titular Christology in the Gospel of Mark*. Journal for the Study of the New Testament Supplement Series 175. Sheffield: Sheffield Academic, 1999.

Church of England. *The Alternative Service Book 1980*. Services authorized for use in the Church of England in conjunction with the Book of Common Prayer. Oxford: Oxford University Press, 1980.

Collins, Adele Yarbro. *Mark: A Commentary*. Hermeneia. Minneapolis: Fortress, 2007.

Crossan, John Dominic. "Mark and the Relatives of Jesus." *Novum Testamentum* 15 (1973) 81–113.

Culpepper, R. Alan. *Mark*. Smyth & Helwys Bible Commentary. Macon, GA: Smyth & Helwys, 2007.

Donahue, John R. *The Theology and Setting of Discipleship in the Gospel of Mark*. Père Marquette Theology Lecture. Milwaukee: Marquette University Press, 1983.

Eliot, T. S. *The Complete Poems and Plays of T. S. Eliot*. London: Faber & Faber, 1969.

Evans, Craig A. *Mark 8:27—16:20*. Word Biblical Commentary 34b. Nashville: Thomas Nelson, 2000.

Gamble, Harry Y. *Books and Readers in the Early Church: A History of Early Christian Texts*. New Haven: Yale University Press, 1995.

———. "Codex." In *The Anchor Bible Dictionary*, edited by David Noel Freedman, 1:1067–69. New York: Doubleday, 1992.

Hengel, Martin. *Studies in the Gospel of Mark*. Translated by John Bowden. London: SCM, 1985.

Bibliography

Hooker, Morna D. *The Gospel According to Saint Mark*. Black's New Testament Commentaries 2. Peabody, MA: Hendrickson, 1991.

Kelber, Werner H. *Mark's Story of Jesus*. Philadelphia: Fortress, 1979.

Kingsbury, Jack Dean. *Conflict in Mark: Jesus, Authorities, Disciples*. Minneapolis: Fortress, 1989.

Lane, William L. *The Gospel of Mark*. New International Commentary on the New Testament. Grand Rapids: Eerdmans, 1974.

Marcus, Joel. *Mark 1–8*. Anchor Bible 27. New York: Doubleday, 2000.

———. *Mark 8–16*. Anchor Bible 27a. New York: Doubleday, 2009.

Metzger, Bruce M. *A Textual Commentary on the Greek New Testament*. 2nd ed. Stuttgart: Deutsche Bibelgesellschaft, 1994.

Moloney, Francis J. *The Gospel of Mark: A Commentary*. Peabody: Hendrickson, 2002.

Petersen, Norman R. *Literary Criticism for New Testament Critics*. Guides to Biblical Scholarship: New Testament Series. Philadelphia: Fortress, 1978.

———. "When Is the End Not the End? Literary Reflections on the Ending of Mark's Narrative." *Interpretation* 34 (1980) 151–66.

Smith, Barbara H. *Poetic Closure: A Study of How Poems End*. Chicago: University of Chicago Press, 1968.

Taylor, Vincent. *The Gospel According to St. Mark*. London: MacMillan, 1953.

Weeden, Theodore J. *Mark—Traditions in Conflict*. Philadelphia: Fortress, 1971.

Whiston, William, translator. *The New Complete Works of Josephus*. Rev. ed. Grand Rapids: Kregel, 1999.

Wrede, William. *The Messianic Secret*. Translated by J. C. G. Grieg. Library of Theological Translations. Cambridge: Clarke, 1971.

www.ingramcontent.com/pod-product-compliance
Lightning Source LLC
Chambersburg PA
CBHW072150160426
43197CB00012B/2320